casual cooking

Let's veg out

casual cooking

Let's veg out

LOVE FOOD™

This edition published by Parragon Books Ltd in 2015
LOVE FOOD is an imprint of Parragon Books Ltd

Parragon Books Ltd
Chartist House
15–17 Trim Street
Bath BA1 1HA, UK
www.parragon.com/lovefood

ISBN 978-1-4723-8490-4

Printed in China

Cover photography by Charlie Richards
Designed by Beth Kalynka
Nutritional analysis by Judith Wills

Notes for the Reader
This book uses both metric and imperial measurements. Follow the same units of measurement
throughout; do not mix metric and imperial. All spoon measurements are level: teaspoons are
assumed to be 5 ml, and tablespoons are assumed to be 15 ml. Unless otherwise stated, milk is
assumed to be full fat, eggs and individual vegetables are medium, and pepper is freshly ground
black pepper. Unless otherwise stated, all root vegetables should be peeled prior to using.

Garnishes, decorations and serving suggestions are all optional and not necessarily included
in the recipe ingredients or method. Any optional ingredients and seasoning to taste are
not included in the nutritional analysis. The times given are an approximate guide only.
Preparation times differ according to the techniques used by different people and the
cooking times may also vary from those given. Optional ingredients, variations or serving
suggestions have not been included in the time calculations. Nutritional values are per
serving (Serves…) or per item (Makes…).

Vegetarians should be aware that some of the ready-made ingredients used in the recipes in this
book may contain animal products. Always check the packaging before use.

contents

rise & shine

Breakfast is one of the most important meals of the day – and it is delicious too! Many of these recipes can be prepared ahead of time – ideal for a busy weekday breakfast. There are also recipes for a lazy weekend brunch, perfect with fresh coffee!

breakfast & brunch

honey & rosemary roast plums

prep: 20 mins, plus cooling
cook: 25–35 mins

350 g/12 oz firm ripe red plums
3–4 fresh rosemary sprigs
6 tbsp clear honey
finely grated zest and juice of ½ orange
100 ml/3½ fl oz double cream
150 ml/5 fl oz Greek-style yogurt
60 g/2¼ oz crunchy muesli

1. Preheat the oven to 190°C/375°F/Gas Mark 5. Halve and stone the plums. Arrange them cut side up in an ovenproof dish large enough to hold them in a single layer. Bruise the rosemary sprigs with a rolling pin and push them among the fruit.

2. Mix together the honey, the orange juice and zest, then pour over the top of the plums.

3. Cover the dish with foil and bake in the preheated oven for 25–35 minutes until the plums are tender. The exact cooking time will depend on the size and ripeness of the fruit. Leave the plums to cool for 15 minutes, then remove the rosemary.

4. Meanwhile, whip the cream until it holds soft peaks. Add the yogurt and gently fold together.

5. To serve, divide the warm plums and their syrupy juices between four bowls. Add a large spoonful of the yogurt mixture to each bowl and sprinkle with the muesli.

variation

To vary the flavour, replace the rosemary with a split vanilla pod or cinnamon sticks.

cals: 361   fat: 18g   sat fat: 9.8g   fibre: 2.8g   carbs: 46g   sugar: 38.6g   salt: trace   protein: 6.5g

fruity granola cups

prep: 25 mins, plus cooling
cook: 30-35 mins

115 g/4 oz granola (see below)

juice of 1 orange

115 g/4 oz Greek-style natural yogurt

1 dessert apple, cored and coarsely grated

115 g/4 oz strawberries, hulled and sliced

40 g/1½ oz blueberries

granola

115 g/4 oz medium oatmeal

85 g/3 oz porridge oats

40 g/1½ oz unblanched almonds, roughly chopped

2 tbsp pumpkin seeds

2 tbsp sunflower seeds

2 tbsp linseeds, coarsely ground

½ tsp ground cinnamon

3 tbsp maple syrup

1 tbsp olive oil

25 g/1 oz goji berries

1. Preheat the oven to 160°C/325°F/Gas Mark 3. To make the granola, put the oatmeal, porridge oats and almonds in a bowl. Stir in the pumpkin seeds, sunflower seeds and linseeds, then the cinnamon, maple syrup and oil.

2. Tip the granola into a roasting tin, then spread into an even layer. Bake for 30-35 minutes, or until golden brown all over, stirring every 5–10 minutes and mixing any browner granola from the edges of the tin into the centre after 15 minutes.

3. Stir in the goji berries, then leave to cool. Pack into an airtight container and store in the refrigerator for up to five days.

4. When ready to serve, spoon the granola into two glasses or bowls, keeping a little back for the top. Moisten with the orange juice. Mix the yogurt with the apple, spoon over the granola, top with the strawberries and blueberries and sprinkle with the remaining granola.

variation

To vary the flavour, replace the rosemary with a split vanilla pod or cinnamon sticks.

cals: 361   fat: 18g   sat fat: 9.8g   fibre: 2.8g   carbs: 46g   sugar: 38.6g   salt: trace   protein: 6.5g

fruity granola cups

prep: 25 mins, plus cooling
cook: 30-35 mins

115 g/4 oz granola (see below)

juice of 1 orange

115 g/4 oz Greek-style natural yogurt

1 dessert apple, cored and coarsely grated

115 g/4 oz strawberries, hulled and sliced

40 g/1½ oz blueberries

granola

115 g/4 oz medium oatmeal

85 g/3 oz porridge oats

40 g/1½ oz unblanched almonds, roughly chopped

2 tbsp pumpkin seeds

2 tbsp sunflower seeds

2 tbsp linseeds, coarsely ground

½ tsp ground cinnamon

3 tbsp maple syrup

1 tbsp olive oil

25 g/1 oz goji berries

1. Preheat the oven to 160°C/325°F/Gas Mark 3. To make the granola, put the oatmeal, porridge oats and almonds in a bowl. Stir in the pumpkin seeds, sunflower seeds and linseeds, then the cinnamon, maple syrup and oil.

2. Tip the granola into a roasting tin, then spread into an even layer. Bake for 30-35 minutes, or until golden brown all over, stirring every 5–10 minutes and mixing any browner granola from the edges of the tin into the centre after 15 minutes.

3. Stir in the goji berries, then leave to cool. Pack into an airtight container and store in the refrigerator for up to five days.

4. When ready to serve, spoon the granola into two glasses or bowls, keeping a little back for the top. Moisten with the orange juice. Mix the yogurt with the apple, spoon over the granola, top with the strawberries and blueberries and sprinkle with the remaining granola.

cals: 196   fat: 0.6g   sat fat: 0.1g   fibre: 6.1g   carbs: 50.3g   sugar: 40g   salt: 0.1g   protein: 3g

oatmeal crunch

prep: 15 mins
cook: 10 mins

100 g/3½ oz rolled oats

450 ml/16 fl oz water

small pinch of salt

2 tbsp chopped ready-to-eat dried apricots

2 tbsp toasted flaked almonds

4 tsp sunflower seeds

1. Mix the oats with the water and salt in a non-stick saucepan and stir well. Bring to the boil over a medium–high heat, stirring occasionally, then reduce the heat and simmer, continuing to stir occasionally, for 5 minutes.

2. When the porridge is thick and creamy, spoon into two serving bowls and top with the apricots, almonds and sunflower seeds. Serve immediately.

serves 2

cals: 340   fat: 13.6g   sat fat: 1.4g   fibre: 8g   carbs: 45.6g   sugar: 8.1g   salt: 1.5g   protein: 12.9g

muesli muffins

prep: 20 mins, plus cooling
cook: 20 mins

140 g/5 oz plain flour
1 tbsp baking powder
280 g/10 oz unsweetened muesli
115 g/4 oz soft light brown sugar
2 eggs
250 ml/9 fl oz buttermilk
6 tbsp sunflower oil

1. Preheat the oven to 200°C/400°F/Gas Mark 6. Place 12 paper muffin cases in a muffin tin.

2. Sift together the flour and baking powder into a large bowl. Stir in the muesli and sugar.

3. Place the eggs in a large jug or bowl and beat lightly. Beat in the buttermilk and oil.

4. Make a well in the centre of the dry ingredients and pour in the beaten liquid ingredients. Stir gently until just combined; do not over-mix. Spoon the mixture into the paper cases.

5. Bake in the preheated oven for about 20 minutes, or until well risen, golden brown and firm to the touch. Leave to cool in the tin for 5 minutes, then serve warm or transfer to a wire rack to cool.

cals: 265   fat: 12g   sat fat: 2.3g   fibre: 3.2g   carbs: 34.3g   sugar: 13.4g   salt: 0.4g   protein: 6.5g

spicy polenta with poached eggs

prep: 25 mins, plus cooling
cook: 25 mins

oil, for oiling

600 ml/1 pint water

150 g/5½ oz polenta

85 g/3 oz freshly grated vegetarian Parmesan-style cheese

40 g/1½ oz butter

½–1 red chilli, deseeded and very finely chopped

200 g/7 oz baby spinach leaves, or a mixture of baby spinach leaves and rocket leaves

2 tsp white wine vinegar

4 large eggs

salt and pepper

1. Lightly oil an 18-cm/7-inch square cake tin. Bring the water to the boil in a saucepan. Add the polenta in a thin stream and cook, stirring, over a medium–low heat for 3 minutes until thick.

2. Stir in 55 g/2 oz of the cheese, 30 g/1 oz of the butter and the chilli. Working quickly, transfer to the prepared tin and level the surface. Set aside for 30 minutes until cool and firm, then cut out four rounds with a 9-cm/3½-inch cutter and transfer to a baking sheet.

3. Wash the spinach and place in a large saucepan with the water clinging to the leaves. Cover and cook for 2–3 minutes until wilted, then squeeze out the excess water between two plates. Return to the pan.

4. Preheat the grill to high. Sprinkle the polenta rounds with the remaining cheese, place under the preheated grill and cook for 3 minutes until brown and bubbling on the top. Keep warm. Meanwhile, add the remaining butter and salt and pepper to taste to the spinach and heat through.

5. Half fill a saucepan with water, add the vinegar and bring to simmering point. Crack the eggs into cups and slide gently into the water. Cook over a low heat, without allowing the water to boil, for 3 minutes until the whites are firm and the yolk is still soft. Scoop out with a slotted spoon and drain briefly on kitchen paper.

6. To serve, place the polenta rounds on four warmed plates and divide the spinach between them. Top with the eggs and season with a little salt and pepper. Serve immediately.

fact

Eggs are ideally packaged to support new life, and so contain all the nutrients we need for growth.

cals: 307   fat: 21.8g   sat fat: 10.8g   fibre: 2g   carbs: 10g   sugar: 0.9g   salt: 2.1g   protein: 17.9g

asparagus & egg pastries

prep: 25 mins, plus chilling
cook: 25–28 mins

500 g/1 lb 2 oz ready-made puff pastry
flour, for dusting
milk, for brushing
300 g/10½ oz slim asparagus spears
200 g/7 oz ready-made vegetarian
   tomato pasta sauce
1 tsp hot smoked paprika
4 eggs
salt and pepper

top tip

These pastries are delicious with some vegetarian Cheddar cheese grated over the top before they are cooked.

1. Roll out the pastry on a lightly floured surface to a 35 x 20-cm/14 x 8-inch rectangle, then cut into four pieces to make four 20 x 9-cm/8 x 3½-inch rectangles. Line a baking sheet with non-stick baking paper and place the pastry rectangles on the tray. Prick all over with a fork and brush lightly with milk. Chill for 20 minutes.

2. Snap the woody ends off the asparagus and discard. Bring a saucepan of lightly salted water to the boil, then add the asparagus, bring back to the boil and cook for 2–3 minutes until almost tender. Drain and refresh in cold water, then drain again.

3. Meanwhile, preheat the oven to 200°C/400°F/Gas Mark 6. Mix the tomato sauce and paprika together and divide between the pastry bases, spreading it out almost to the edges. Bake in the preheated oven for 10–12 minutes until the pastry is puffed around the edges and pale golden in colour.

4. Remove from the oven and arrange the asparagus on top, leaving space for the egg in the middle of each pastry. Crack one egg into a cup and slide into the space created in one of the pastries. Repeat with the remaining eggs, then return the pastries to the oven for 8 minutes, or until the eggs are just set. Season with salt and pepper and serve immediately.

cals: 605   fat: 36g   sat fat: 16.8g   fibre: 5.3g   carbs: 52.7g   sugar: 6.3g   salt: 2.4g   protein: 17.2g

courgette fritters

prep: 25 mins
cook: 30-40 mins

85 g/3 oz brown rice flour
1 tsp baking powder
2 eggs, beaten
200 ml/7 fl oz milk
250 g/9 oz courgettes
2 tbsp fresh thyme leaves
1 tbsp virgin olive oil
salt and pepper

1. Sift the flour and baking powder into a large bowl, then tip the remaining bran in the sieve into the bowl. Make a well in the centre. Pour the eggs into the well and, using a wooden spoon, gradually draw in the flour. Slowly pour in the milk, stirring continuously to form a thick batter.

2. Meanwhile, place kitchen paper on a plate and grate the courgettes over it so it absorbs some of the juices.

3. Pat the courgettes dry, then add them and the thyme to the batter, season with salt and pepper and mix well.

4. Heat the oil in a frying pan over a medium-high heat. Drop tablespoons of the batter into the pan, leaving a little space between them. Cook in batches for 3–4 minutes on each side, or until golden brown.

5. Line a baking sheet with kitchen paper. Transfer the fritters to the baking sheet using a slotted spoon and let them drain well. Remove the kitchen paper and keep each batch warm while you make the rest. Allow five fritters per person and serve immediately.

cals: 155   fat: 6.8g   sat fat: 1.9g   fibre: 1.5g   carbs: 17.2g   sugar: 3.5g   salt: 1.6g   protein: 6g

pancakes with baked mushrooms

prep: 25 mins, plus standing
cook: 20 mins

150 g/5½ oz plain white flour
1½ tsp baking powder
pinch of salt
250 ml/8½ fl oz milk
1 large egg
2 tbsp melted butter
sunflower oil, for greasing

topping
55 g/2 oz butter
2 tbsp chopped fresh parsley
1 tbsp snipped chives
1 garlic clove, crushed
3 tbsp olive oil
12 field mushrooms
salt and pepper

variation

For a sweet version of this recipe, these pancakes are also delicious topped with fresh fruit and honey.

1. To make the topping, preheat the oven to 200°C/400°F/Gas Mark 6. Beat the butter until softened, stir in the parsley and chives and season to taste with salt and pepper.

2. Mix the garlic and oil together. Place the mushrooms on a baking sheet in a single layer, brush with the garlic oil and season with salt and pepper to taste. Bake in the oven for about 15 minutes, turning once, until tender.

3. Meanwhile, sift the flour, baking powder and salt into a bowl. Add the milk, egg and butter and whisk to a smooth batter. Leave to stand for 5 minutes.

4. Lightly grease a griddle pan or frying pan and heat over a medium heat. Spoon tablespoons of batter onto the pan and cook until bubbles appear on the surface.

5. Turn over with a palette knife and cook the other side until golden brown. Repeat this process using the remaining batter, while keeping the cooked pancakes warm.

6. Place a mushroom on each pancake, top with a spoonful of herb butter and serve immediately.

serves 6

cals: 344   fat: 22.6g   sat fat: 9.6g   fibre: 3g   carbs: 28.2g   sugar: 6.4g   salt: 1.7g   protein: 9g

balancing act

Eating a wide variety of foods every day is the best way to ensure you get all the nutrients that you need naturally. Vegetarians, just like meat-eaters, need a variety of nutrients on a daily basis in order to function in tip-top form and remain healthy. It's all about eating a well-balanced diet.

Proteins

These are essential for healthy growth and repair of cells. They are also needed for protection against infection and building up resistance. The daily requirement is small and the main natural sources of protein are:

Dairy – eggs, cheese, yogurt and milk.

Cereals – rice, oats, corn, wheat and flour products, pasta, couscous, barley and rye.

Pulses – dried beans including soya and soya bean products (such as tofu), chickpeas and lentils.

Seeds and nuts – walnuts, Brazil nuts, pecan nuts, almonds, cashew nuts, pine nuts, peanuts and peanut butter; pumpkin seeds, sunflower seeds, linseeds, sesame seeds and tahini paste.

Carbohydrates

These are needed for energy. They can either be simple or complex, and it is the complex carbohydrates that are most nutritionally beneficial as they contain a mix of vitamins and minerals, and release the energy you need slowly. Good sources are almost all fruit and vegetables, especially root vegetables, potatoes, bananas; pulses; and whole grains, cereals, rice and pasta.

Fats

While we don't want to consume large amounts of fat in our diet, a little is beneficial but it's important to know what type of fat to eat. Saturated fat is known as 'bad' fat. Most of the fat derived from animal products is 'bad' fat because of the links with serious diseases.

'Good' fats, which are called polyunsaturated or monounsaturated, come from vegetable plants, for example olive and sunflower oils, and these are the ones you should use in cooking and salad dressings.

Most fruits and vegetables are very low in saturated fat, which is good news for a vegetarian diet. Avocados, olives, nuts and seeds also contain the 'good' fats.

What is a serving?

Eating five or more servings of fruit and vegetables every day is important. One serving is equal to:

100 ml/3½ fl oz fruit juice (only one glass a day counts).

1 medium fruit or vegetable, such as an apple, orange or onion.

3 heaped tablespoons of fresh or canned fruit salad, sliced carrots or mushrooms or cooked lentils.

1 tablespoon of raisins or sultanas, 4 dried apricots, or a handful of banana chips.

healthy breakfast frittata

prep: 20 mins
cook: 20 mins

250 g/9 oz baby new potatoes,
  unpeeled and sliced
2 tbsp virgin olive oil
4 spring onions, thinly sliced
1 courgette, thinly sliced
115 g/4 oz baby spinach, destalked
large pinch of smoked hot paprika
6 eggs
salt and pepper

1. Bring a saucepan of water to the boil, add the potatoes and cook for 5 minutes, or until just tender, then drain well.

2. Meanwhile, heat 1 tablespoon of oil in a large ovenproof frying pan over a medium heat. Add the spring onions, courgette and potatoes and fry, stirring and turning the vegetables, for 5 minutes, or until just beginning to brown.

3. Add the spinach and paprika and cook, stirring, for 1–2 minutes, or until the leaves have just wilted.

4. Preheat the grill to medium-high. Crack the eggs into a bowl and season with salt and pepper. Beat lightly with a fork until evenly mixed. Pour a little extra oil into the pan if needed, then pour in the eggs and cook for 5–6 minutes, or until they are almost set and the underside of the frittata is golden brown.

5. Grill the frittata for 3–4 minutes, or until the top is browned and the eggs are set. Cut into wedges and serve.

top tip

If you have cooked new potatoes left over from last night's supper in the refrigerator, use these rather than cooking more.

5

cals: 245   fat: 15g   sat fat: 3.6g   fibre: 3.3g   carbs: 14.6g   sugar: 2.8g   salt: 1.9g   protein: 13.4g

bagels with leeks & cheese

prep: 15 mins, plus cooling
cook: 12–15 mins

2 fresh bagels, halved

25 g/1 oz butter

2 leeks, finely sliced

125 g/4½ oz freshly grated vegetarian
    Parmesan-style cheese

2 spring onions, finely chopped

1 tbsp chopped fresh parsley

salt and pepper

1. Preheat the grill to a medium setting. Lay the bagels cut side up on the rack in the grill pan. Toast until lightly browned, then reserve and keep warm. Do not turn the grill off.

2. Melt the butter over a low heat in a large sauté pan and add the leeks. Cook, stirring constantly, for 5 minutes, or until the leeks are soft and slightly browned. Leave to cool.

3. Mix together the cooled leeks, grated cheese, spring onions, parsley and salt and pepper to taste. Spread the cheese mixture over the top of each bagel and place under the grill until bubbling and golden brown.

variation

Bagels come in a variety of different flavours – choose one with a tasty topping like poppy seeds for extra crunch.

serves 2

cals: 686   fat: 28.2g   sat fat: 17g   fibre: 4.7g   carbs: 72.5g   sugar: 4.3g   salt: 5.6g   protein: 35.2g

mushroom bruschetta

prep: 15-20 mins
cook: 8 mins

12 slices baguette, each 1 cm/½ inch
 thick, or 2 individual baguettes,
 cut lengthways

3 tbsp olive oil

2 garlic cloves, crushed

225 g/8 oz chestnut mushrooms, sliced

225 g/8 oz mixed wild mushrooms

2 tsp lemon juice

2 tbsp chopped fresh parsley

salt and pepper

1. Preheat the grill to medium–high. Place the slices of baguette on a ridged griddle pan and toast on both sides until golden. Reserve and keep warm.

2. Meanwhile, heat the oil in a frying pan. Add the garlic and cook gently for a few seconds, then add the chestnut mushrooms. Cook, stirring constantly, over a high heat for 3 minutes. Add the wild mushrooms and cook for a further 2 minutes. Stir in the lemon juice.

3. Season to taste with salt and pepper and stir in the chopped parsley.

4. Spoon the mushroom mixture onto the warm toast and serve immediately.

serves 4

top tip

Look out for packs of mixed mushrooms that are ideal for this recipe.

cals: 303   fat: 14.2g   sat fat: 2.1g   fibre: 3.4g   carbs: 37.5g   sugar: 1.4g   salt: 2.1g   protein: 8.3g

cinnamon swirls

prep: 35 mins, plus rising and cooling
cook: 20-30 mins

225 g/8 oz strong white flour

½ tsp salt

2 tsp easy-blend dried yeast

25 g/1 oz butter, cut into small pieces,
plus extra for greasing

1 egg, lightly beaten

125 ml/4 fl oz warm milk

2 tbsp maple syrup, for glazing

filling

55 g/2 oz tbsp butter, softened

2 tsp ground cinnamon

50 g/1¾ oz soft light brown sugar

50 g/1¾ oz currants

1. Grease a baking sheet with a little butter.

2. Sift the flour and salt into a mixing bowl. Stir in the yeast. Rub in the butter with your fingertips until the mixture resembles breadcrumbs. Add the egg and milk and mix to form a dough.

3. Form the dough into a ball, place in a greased bowl, cover and leave to stand in a warm place for about 40 minutes, or until doubled in size.

4. Lightly knock back the dough for 1 minute, then roll out to a rectangle measuring 30 x 23 cm/12 x 9 inches.

5. To make the filling, cream together the butter, cinnamon and sugar until light and fluffy. Spread the filling evenly over the dough rectangle, leaving a 2.5-cm/1-inch border all around. Sprinkle the currants evenly over the top.

6. Roll up the dough from one of the long edges, and press down to seal. Cut the roll into 12 slices. Place them, cut-side down, on the baking sheet, cover and leave to stand for 30 minutes.

7. Meanwhile, preheat the oven to 190°C/375°F/Gas Mark 5. Bake the buns in the preheated oven for 20–30 minutes, or until well risen. Brush with the maple syrup and leave to cool slightly before serving.

makes 12

cals: 174   fat: 7.1g   sat fat: 4.2g   fibre: 1.1g   carbs: 23.7g   sugar: 9.7g   salt: 0.4g   protein: 4.3g

fresh croissants

prep: 45-55 mins, plus rising and chilling
cook: 20-25 mins

500 g/1 lb 2 oz strong white bread
flour, plus extra for rolling

40 g/1½ oz caster sugar

1 tsp salt

2 tsp easy-blend dried yeast

300 ml/10 fl oz milk, heated until just
warm to the touch

300 g/10½ oz butter, softened,
plus extra for greasing

1 egg, lightly beaten with 1 tbsp milk,
for glazing

strawberry jam, to serve (optional)

1. Stir the dry ingredients into a large bowl,
make a well in the centre and add the milk.
Mix to a soft dough, adding more milk if
too dry. Knead on a lightly floured work
surface for 5–10 minutes, or until smooth
and elastic. Leave to rise in a large greased
bowl, covered, in a warm place until doubled
in size.

2. Meanwhile, flatten the butter with
a rolling pin between two sheets of
greaseproof paper to form a rectangle about
5 mm/¼ inch thick, then chill.

3. Knead the dough for 1 minute. Remove
the butter from the refrigerator and leave
to soften slightly.

4. Roll out the dough on a well-floured work
surface to a rectangle 46 x 15 cm/18 x 6
inches. Place the butter in the centre, folding
up the sides and squeezing the edges together
gently. With the short end of the dough
towards you, fold the top third down towards
the centre, then fold the bottom third up.
Rotate 90° clockwise so that the fold is to
your left and the top flap towards your right.
Roll out to a rectangle and fold again. If the
butter feels soft, wrap the dough in clingfilm
and chill. Repeat the rolling process twice
more. Cut the dough in half. Roll out one
half into a triangle 5 mm/¼ inch thick (keep
the other half refrigerated). Use a cardboard
triangular template, base 18 cm/7 inches and
sides 20 cm/8 inches, to cut out six croissants.
Repeat with the other half of the dough.

5. Preheat the oven to 200°C/400°F/Gas
Mark 6. Brush the triangles lightly with the
glaze. Roll into croissant shapes, starting at
the base and tucking the point underneath
to prevent unrolling while cooking. Brush
again with the glaze. Place on an ungreased
baking sheet and leave to double in size. Bake
for 15–20 minutes until golden brown. Serve
warm with jam, if liked.

makes 12

cals: 374   fat: 22.2g   sat fat: 13.6g   fibre: 1.2g   carbs: 35.2g   sugar: 5.1g   salt: 1g   protein: 8.5g

cinnamon pancakes with fruit salad

prep: 30 mins
cook: 25 mins

100 g/3½ oz wholemeal plain flour

½ tsp ground cinnamon

2 eggs, beaten

225 ml/8 fl oz unsweetened soya milk

3 tbsp water

3 tbsp sunflower oil

fruit salad

1 ruby grapefruit

250 g/9 oz pineapple flesh, cut into cubes

150 g/5½ oz mango flesh, cut into cubes

finely grated zest of ½ lime

to serve (optional)

300 g/10½ oz natural soya yogurt

2 tbsp date syrup

1. To make the fruit salad, cut the peel and pith away from the grapefruit with a small serrated knife. Hold it above a bowl and cut between the membranes to release the segments. Squeeze the juice from the membranes into the bowl. Add the pineapple, mango and lime zest and mix well.

2. To make the pancakes, put the flour and cinnamon in another bowl. Add the eggs, then gradually whisk in the soya milk until smooth. Whisk in the water and 1 tablespoon of oil.

3. Heat a little oil in an 18-cm/7-inch frying pan over a medium heat, then pour out the excess oil. Pour in one-eighth of the batter, tilting the pan to swirl the batter into an even layer. Cook for 2 minutes, or until the underside is golden.

4. Loosen the pancake, then flip it over with a palette knife and cook the second side for 1 minute, or until golden. Slide out of the pan and keep hot on a plate while you make seven more thin pancakes in the same way.

5. Arrange two folded pancakes on each of four plates and top with the fruit salad. Serve with a spoonful of the yogurt, drizzled with the date syrup, if liked.

cals: 313   fat: 14.8g   sat fat: 2.3g   fibre: 5.7g   carbs: 39g   sugar: 15.8g   salt: 0.1g   protein: 6.8g

banana breakfast shake

2 large ripe bananas
2 tbsp oat bran
2 tbsp honey
1 tbsp lemon juice
300 ml/10 fl oz soya milk
ground cinnamon, to serve (optional)

1. Roughly chop the bananas and place in a large jug with the oat bran, honey and lemon juice. Add the soya milk.

2. Blend the ingredients with an electric hand-held blender, or tip into a food processor or blender and process until smooth and bubbly.

3. Pour the shake into tall glasses and sprinkle with cinnamon, if liked. Serve immediately.

top tip

If you don't have a blender, simply mash the bananas with a fork and then combine with the remaining ingredients.

cals: 259   fat: 3.8g   sat fat: 0.7g   fibre: 6g   carbs: 55.7g   sugar: 34.4g   salt: trace   protein: 8.3g

mango & lime juice

prep: 15-20 mins
cook: no cooking

1 tbsp sesame seeds

½ lime, juice squeezed

30 g/1 oz green curly kale,
  torn into pieces

1 mango, stoned, peeled and roughly
  chopped

225 ml/8 fl oz unsweetened rice,
  almond or soya milk

small handful of crushed ice

1. Put the sesame seeds in a blender and whizz until finely ground. Add the lime juice, kale and mango and whizz until blended.

2. Add the milk and crushed ice and whizz again until smooth.

3. Pour into a glass and serve immediately.

fact

Most of us don't eat enough green vegetables and the kale in this juice is an easy way to increase your consumption.

1

serves 1

cals: 346   fat: 10g   sat fat: 1.7g   fibre: 8.5g   carbs: 57.6g   sugar: 46.4g   salt: 0.1g   protein: 11g

on the go

Invest in some good-quality plastic containers so that you can take soups and salads to work for lunch. It will save money and you'll know exactly what ingredients have gone into it. Tarts and frittatas are also great for lunches or for family picnics!

the big freeze

It is said that frozen vegetables are often more nutritious than fresh as they are frozen very shortly after harvesting, when nutrients are at their peak. Most supermarkets stock a wide range of frozen veggies so next time you are shopping have a look.

let's do lunch

winter vegetable soup

2 tbsp vegetable oil

1 large onion, thickly sliced

1 large potato, cut into chunks

3 celery sticks, thickly sliced

4 carrots, sliced

175 g/6 oz swede, cut into chunks

4 large garlic cloves, peeled and left whole

1.5 litres/2½ pints vegetable stock

225 g/8 oz canned chopped tomatoes

1 leek, halved lengthways and thickly sliced

salt and pepper

2 tbsp chopped fresh flat-leaf parsley, to garnish

grated vegetarian Cheddar cheese, to serve (optional)

1. Heat the oil in a large, heavy-based saucepan over a medium heat. Add the onion, potato, celery, carrots, swede and garlic cloves. Season to taste with salt and pepper, then cover and cook over a medium heat, stirring occasionally, for 10 minutes.

2. Pour in the stock and tomatoes and bring to the boil. Reduce the heat and simmer, partially covered, for 30 minutes. Add the leek and cook for a further 5 minutes, until just tender.

3. Taste and adjust the seasoning, adding salt and pepper if needed. Ladle into warmed bowls, garnish with the parsley and serve immediately with grated cheese, if liked.

variation

Add some small soup pasta to the pan for a heartier meal. Cook according to package instructions.

lentil & chard soup

prep: 20-25 mins
cook: 50 mins

150 g/5½ oz brown lentils

1 onion, finely diced

400 ml/14 fl oz passata

600–750 ml/1–1¼ pints vegetable stock

½ tsp cumin seeds, lightly crushed, plus extra to garnish

350 g/12 oz chard

175 g/6 oz potatoes, cut into 1-cm/½-inch cubes

6 tbsp chopped fresh mint

2 wholemeal pittas

6 tbsp Greek-style yogurt

salt and pepper

lemon wedges, to garnish

fact

Swiss chard is similar to spinach and beets, sharing the same bitter and slightly salty taste.

1. Put the lentils in a large saucepan with the onion, passata, 600 ml/1 pint of the stock, the ½ teaspoon cumin seeds and ½ teaspoon salt. Bring to the boil, then cover and simmer over a low heat for 20 minutes, until the lentils are just tender.

2. Remove the stems from the chard leaves and thinly slice. Slice the leaves crossways into ribbons.

3. Add the chard stems and potatoes to the lentils and cook for 10 minutes.

4. Add the chard leaves and cook for a further 15 minutes. If necessary, add the remaining stock to thin the soup – but it should still be quite thick. Stir in 4 tablespoons of the mint and season to taste with salt and pepper.

5. Meanwhile, preheat the grill to medium. Open out the pittas and toast under the preheated grill for 3 minutes, until crisp. Break into bite-sized pieces and arrange around the edge of six soup plates.

6. Ladle the soup into the plates. Add 1 tablespoon of yogurt to each and sprinkle with the remaining mint and cumin seeds. Garnish with lemon wedges and serve immediately.

serves 6

cals: 232   fat: 2.6g   sat fat: 1.2g   fibre: 12.3g   carbs: 42g   sugar: 6.7g   salt: 3.4g   protein: 12.9g

roast squash soup

prep: 25-30 mins
cook: 1-1¼ hours

1 kg/2 lb 4 oz butternut squash, peeled, deseeded and cut into small chunks

2 onions, cut into wedges

2 tbsp olive oil

2 garlic cloves, crushed

3–4 fresh thyme sprigs, leaves removed

1 litre/1¾ pints vegetable stock

150 ml/5 fl oz crème fraîche

salt and pepper

snipped fresh chives, to garnish

cheese toasties

1 baguette, thinly sliced diagonally

40 g/1½ oz vegetarian hard cheese, grated

1. Preheat the oven to 190°C/375°F/Gas Mark 5. Place the squash, onions, oil, garlic and thyme in a roasting tin. Toss together and spread out in a single layer.

2. Roast in the preheated oven for 50–60 minutes, stirring occasionally, until the vegetables are tender and slightly caramelized.

3. Transfer the vegetables to a saucepan. Add half the stock and purée with a hand-held blender until smooth. Stir in the remaining stock and crème fraîche. Season to taste with salt and pepper, and heat through gently.

4. To make the toasties, preheat the grill to high. Toast the sliced baguette under the preheated grill for 1–2 minutes on each side until pale golden. Sprinkle with the cheese and return to the grill for a further 30–40 seconds, until melted and bubbling. Ladle the soup into warmed bowls and sprinkle with chives. Serve immediately with the toasties.

serves 4

top tip

Chop the butternut squash into similar-sized chunks to ensure even cooking.

cals: 381   fat: 25.3g   sat fat: 11.5g   fibre: 7g   carbs: 54.7g   sugar: 10g   salt: 3.6g   protein: 9.5g

roasted beetroot & farro salad

prep: 20-25 mins
cook: 30-40 mins

2 raw beetroot (approx 175 g/6 oz), quartered

3 sprigs of fresh thyme

5 tbsp walnut oil

100 g/3½ oz quick-cook farro, rinsed

1 large red pepper, halved lengthways and deseeded

25 g/1 oz walnuts, roughly chopped

85 g/3 oz rocket leaves

thick balsamic vinegar, for drizzling

salt and pepper

variation

While farro is delicious, this salad works equally well with barley instead. The barley will need boiling for 35 minutes.

1. Preheat the oven to 190°C/375°F/Gas Mark 5. Preheat the grill to high. Cut out two squares of foil.

2. Divide the beetroot and thyme between the foil squares. Sprinkle with a little of the oil and season with salt and pepper. Wrap in a loose parcel, sealing the edges, and place on a baking sheet. Roast for 30–40 minutes, or until tender.

3. Meanwhile, put the farro in a saucepan, cover with water and add ½ teaspoon of salt. Bring to the boil, then reduce the heat, cover and simmer for 20 minutes, or according to the pack instructions, until the grains are tender. Drain the farro and tip it into a dish.

4. Meanwhile, put the red pepper halves, cut-side down, on the grill pan and grill for 10 minutes, or until blackened. Cover with a clean tea-towel and leave to stand for 10 minutes. Remove and discard the skin and roughly chop the flesh.

5. Divide the cooked farro between four plates. Slice the beetroot quarters in half, arrange on top of the farro and toss. Scatter over the red pepper, walnuts and rocket.

6. Drizzle with the remaining oil and some balsamic vinegar. Serve immediately.

serves 4

cals: 318   fat: 21.8g   sat fat: 2g   fibre: 4.4g   carbs: 26.7g   sugar: 5.6g   salt: 1.6g   protein: 5.6g

watermelon & goat's cheese salad

prep: 20-25 mins
cook: no cooking

800 g/1 lb 12 oz watermelon flesh, cut into large cubes

grated rind and juice of 2 large limes, plus lime wedges, to serve

½–1 red chilli, deseeded and finely chopped

55 g/2 oz fresh coriander, roughly chopped

70 g/2½ oz rocket

115 g/4 oz firm vegetarian goat's cheese, cut into cubes

salt and pepper

1. Put the watermelon in a large salad bowl. Sprinkle with the lime rind and juice and the chilli, then season with a little salt and pepper and toss gently together.

2. Sprinkle over the coriander, rocket and goat's cheese and gently toss together.

3. Serve with lime wedges.

1

top tip

Look for watermelons that sound hollow when tapped then reveal strong red-coloured flesh inside with no white streaks.

serves 4

cals: 212   fat: 10.8g   sat fat: 7.1g   fibre: 2.6g   carbs: 21.2g   sugar: 14.4g   salt: 1.8g   protein: 11g

cucumber & lamb's lettuce salad

prep: 15-20 mins
cook: no cooking

½ cucumber, diced
100 g/3½ oz lamb's lettuce
4 ripe figs

dressing
1 small shallot, finely chopped
4 tbsp walnut oil
2 tbsp extra virgin olive oil
2 tbsp cider vinegar
½ tsp clear honey
salt and pepper

fact

Figs are really good for you as they contain high amounts of fibre and iron. They are best eaten on the day of purchase though as they deteriorate quite quickly.

1. Place all the dressing ingredients in a screw-top jar, including salt and pepper to taste, and shake well to mix.

2. Put the cucumber and lettuce into a bowl and pour over half the dressing.

3. Toss well to coat evenly, then divide between four serving plates.

4. Cut the figs into quarters and arrange 4 quarters on top of each plate. Drizzle over the remaining dressing and serve immediately.

serves 4

cals: 235 fat: 20.5g sat fat: 2.1g fibre: 1.9g carbs: 12.9g sugar: 9.8g salt: 1.5g protein: 1g

roasted tomato pasta salad

prep: 25 mins, plus cooling
cook: 40 mins

600 g/1 lb 5 oz tomatoes in various colours and sizes, halved

2 garlic cloves, finely chopped

6 tbsp olive oil

225 g/8 oz dried wholewheat pasta, such as mafalda corta or quills

85 g/3 oz baby spinach

salt and pepper

spinach pesto

50 g/1¾ oz fresh basil, plus extra leaves to garnish

25 g/1 oz pine nuts

25 g/1 oz vegetarian Parmesan-style cheese, finely grated, plus cheese shavings to garnish

1. Preheat the oven to 160°C/325°F/Gas Mark 3. Put the tomatoes in a roasting tin, cut side up, add the garlic and 2 tablespoons of olive oil and season with salt and pepper. Roast for 40 minutes, or until softened and just beginning to brown. Leave to cool, then chop up any larger ones.

2. Meanwhile, put the pasta in a large saucepan of boiling water. Bring back to the boil, cover and simmer according to the packet instructions, until just tender. Drain into a colander, rinse with cold water, then drain again.

3. To make the pesto, put all the ingredients in a blender, add 25 g/1 oz baby spinach and the remaining 4 tablespoons of olive oil and whizz until smooth. Season lightly with salt and pepper.

4. Put the pasta and pesto in a salad bowl, toss together, then add the remaining spinach and toss again briefly. Add the tomatoes and any pan juices and toss gently. Garnish with the cheese shavings and basil leaves and serve.

serves 4

cals: 472   fat: 28.3g   sat fat: 4.2g   fibre: 7.9g   carbs: 44.3g   sugar: 6g   salt: 1.8g   protein: 13.4g

tomato & rosemary focaccia

prep: 30 mins, plus rising and cooling
cook: 20 mins

500 g/1 lb 2 oz strong white bread flour, plus extra for dusting

1½ tsp salt

1½ tsp easy-blend dried yeast

2 tbsp chopped fresh rosemary, plus extra sprigs to garnish

6 tbsp extra virgin olive oil, plus extra for brushing

300 ml/10 fl oz lukewarm water

6 oven-dried or sun-blush tomato halves

1 tsp coarse sea salt

1. Sift the flour and 1½ teaspoons salt together into a bowl and stir in the yeast and rosemary. Make a well in the centre, pour in 4 tablespoons of the olive oil and mix quickly with a wooden spoon.

2. Gradually stir in the lukewarm water but do not overmix. Turn out on to a lightly floured surface and knead for 2 minutes. The dough will be wet; do not add more flour.

3. Brush a bowl with oil. Shape the dough into a ball, put it into the bowl and put the bowl into a polythene bag or cover with a damp tea towel. Leave to rise in a warm place for 2 hours, until doubled in volume.

4. Brush a baking sheet with oil. Turn out the dough on to a lightly floured surface and knock back with your fist, then knead for 1 minute. Put the dough on to the prepared baking sheet and press out into an even layer. Put the baking sheet into a polythene bag or cover with a damp tea towel. Leave to rise in a warm place for 1 hour.

5. Preheat the oven to 240°C/475°F/Gas Mark 9. Cut the tomato halves in half. Whisk the remaining oil with a little water in a bowl. Dip your fingers into the oil mixture and press them into the dough to make dimples all over the loaf. Sprinkle with the sea salt. Press the tomato quarters into some of the dimples, drizzle with the remaining oil mixture and sprinkle the loaf with the rosemary sprigs.

6. Lower the oven temperature to 220°C/425°F/Gas Mark 7 and bake the focaccia for 20 minutes, until golden brown. Transfer to a wire rack to cool slightly, then serve while still warm. Alternatively, allow the loaf to cool completely and reheat in a low oven before serving.

cals: 645   fat: 22.3g   sat fat: 3.2g   fibre: 3.9g   carbs: 89.8g   sugar: 2.3g   salt: 4g   protein: 20.2g

grilled vegetable subs

prep: 25-30 mins
cook: 15 mins

1 small aubergine, sliced into
  5-mm/¼-inch rounds

2 garlic cloves, finely chopped

2 tbsp olive oil

2 red, yellow or green peppers,
  deseeded and sliced into rings

1 courgette, sliced lengthways into
  5-mm/¼-inch wide strips

1 red onion, sliced into 5-mm/¼-inch
  wide rings

4 submarine rolls

4 tbsp vegetarian pesto

55 g/2 oz vegetarian Parmesan-style
  cheese, shaved finely

salt and pepper

mixed salad leaves, to serve (optional)

1. Line a large plate with a double layer of kitchen paper. Sprinkle the aubergine rounds with salt. Lay in a single layer on the prepared plate. Put the garlic into a small bowl with the oil and mix to combine.

2. Blot the aubergine dry with kitchen paper, then brush all the vegetables on both sides with the garlic oil and season with pepper. Heat a ridged griddle pan over a high heat and add the vegetables in a single layer. Cook for about 4 minutes on each side, until soft and tender and ridge marks appear.

3. Meanwhile, split the rolls and brush the inside of each with some pesto. Preheat the grill to high.

4. Pile the vegetables onto the bottom half of each roll in layers and top with the cheese. Put the rolls back onto the griddle pan and place under the preheated grill, cheese-side up, and cook for about 2 minutes until the cheese begins to melt. Add the tops of the rolls and serve hot with the salad leaves, if liked.

serves 4

cals: 443   fat: 18.4g   sat fat: 4.5g   fibre: 7.5g   carbs: 55.8g   sugar: 9.4g   salt: 3.4g   protein: 16g

grow your own

If you want to grow your own veg, but have limited space, why not consider growing it in containers? Home-grown vegetables will taste far better than anything you can buy in the shops and you'll also have the satisfaction of knowing you grew it yourself.

veg to grow

Cabbages

Cabbage might not be everyone's choice for growing in the limited space available in a container, but it is considerably more compact than most brassicas, and a number of the red and Savoy cabbages are attractive plants.

Carrots

To grow carrots in containers you need to look for short, thick varieties, rather than the larger winter ones that take longer to mature. Also aim to give the carrots as much depth as possible because they will not grow well in a shallow bag.

Cucumbers

Modern varieties of cucumbers grow well in containers as they are tolerant of lower temperatures. Plant the seeds on their edge directly into the containers, as they do not respond well to being transplanted from smaller pots.

Lettuces

Lettuces mature quickly, require little room and can be grown easily in between other vegetables so they make a fantastic stand-by for the container garden. Sow two seeds in a small degradable pot, using as many small pots as necessary. If both germinate discard the weaker seedling. It may be necessary to harden off the plants by putting them outside during the day before planting them out in their final position outdoors.

Peas

These are great to grow in containers, and should be grown as a feature plant in pots up a decorative trellis. If your pots are on an exposed patio or roof garden they may require protection, both from the wind and birds. Check the height of the variety you choose before planting, this can vary from 46 cm–1.5 m/1½–5 ft.

Radishes

The ordinary globe-shaped summer radish is a great plant to grow in pots alongside lettuces, or it can be used as a filler among containers of brassicas.

Salad leaves

These are good to have in containers just outside your kitchen door so they are within easy reach. They add a lovely peppery flavour to salads.

Spring onions

These can be successfully grown in any containers as they are quick growing and don't take up too much room.

Tomatoes

Dwarf tomatoes, plants that grow little more than 20 cm/8 inches high, are suitable for growing in window boxes and small pots but the yield is not high. Sow two seeds in a small pot and discard the weaker if they both germinate.

mediterranean wrap

1 small courgette, thickly sliced

1 red pepper, halved, deseeded and cut into chunks

1 tbsp olive oil

4 soft flatbreads

6 tbsp sun-dried tomato purée

85 g/3 oz baby spinach, shredded

4 artichoke hearts in oil, drained and quartered

8 sun-dried tomatoes in oil, drained and quartered

16 black olives, stoned and halved

50 g/1¾ oz fresh basil leaves, torn

1. Preheat the oven to 190°C/375°F/Gas Mark 5. Arrange the courgette and pepper on a baking sheet in a single layer, pour over the oil and toss together to coat. Roast for 20 minutes, or until the vegetables have softened and are beginning to brown.

2. Meanwhile, spread each flatbread with a thin layer of sun-dried tomato purée, then top with the spinach.

3. Put the roast vegetables, artichokes, sun-dried tomatoes, olives and basil in a bowl and toss together. Divide the mixture between the flatbreads. Roll the flatbreads up tightly, slice in half and serve.

top tip

These wraps are good with a few slices of vegetarian Cheddar, mozzarella or goat's cheese added in with the vegetables.

cals: 360   fat: 18.3g   sat fat: 5.4g   fibre: 5.8g   carbs: 40.8g   sugar: 7g   salt: 2.1g   protein: 8.5g

falafel pitta pockets

prep: 30 mins
cook: 15-20 mins

2–3 garlic cloves
1 shallot, quartered
425 g/15 oz canned chickpeas
30 g/1 oz fresh flat-leaf parsley leaves
1 tsp ground coriander
1 tsp ground cumin
1½ tsp salt
pinch of cayenne pepper
2 tbsp olive oil
2 tbsp plain flour
½ tsp baking powder
rapeseed oil, for frying

tahini dressing
2 tbsp tahini
juice of 1 lemon
2–3 tbsp water
½ tsp salt
pinch of pepper
pinch of cayenne pepper

pittas and filling
4 pittas
1 romaine lettuce heart
1 large tomato
½ cucumber
Kalamata olives

1. Preheat the oven to 200°C/400°F/Gas Mark 6. Place the garlic in a food processor with the shallot and pulse a few times to chop.

2. Drain and rinse the chickpeas and add to the garlic and shallot mixture. Add the parsley, coriander, cumin, salt, cayenne pepper, olive oil and flour. Process to a chunky purée. Add the baking powder and pulse once to incorporate.

3. To make the dressing, put all the ingredients in a small bowl and stir to combine.

4. Heat 5 mm/¼ inch of rapeseed oil in a large frying pan. Make walnut-sized balls out of the chickpea mixture, and then flatten the balls into 5-mm/¼-inch thick patties. Wrap the pittas in foil and place in the preheated oven.

5. When the oil is hot, add several patties to the pan and fry them for about 1½–2 minutes on each side until well browned.

6. Transfer to a plate lined with kitchen paper to drain. Repeat with the remaining patties until they have all been fried.

7. Shred the lettuce and slice the tomato and cucumber. Remove the pittas from the oven and slice them in half.

8. Stuff each half with 2–3 patties, drizzle with the dressing and fill with lettuce, tomato slices and cucumber slices. Serve 2 halves per person with olives alongside.

top tip

The falafel mixture can be made up to 2 days in advance. Store it covered in the refrigerator.

serves 4

cals: 464   fat: 20.1g   sat fat: 2.3g   fibre: 5.7g   carbs: 58.2g   sugar: 2.4g   salt: 4g   protein: 13.3g

white bean & tomato bruschetta

prep: 25 mins
cook: 5 mins

800 g/1 lb 12 oz canned cannellini beans, drained and rinsed

1 garlic clove, crushed

2 tbsp extra virgin olive oil, plus extra for drizzling

1 tsp lemon juice

1 tbsp chopped fresh flat-leaf parsley

¾ tsp chopped fresh rosemary leaves

25 g/1 oz rocket

8 slices sourdough bread

16 baby plum tomatoes, quartered lengthways

salt and pepper

1. Combine the beans, garlic, oil, lemon juice, parsley and rosemary in a large bowl. Season to taste with sea salt and pepper, then mash to a chunky purée with a fork.

2. Roughly chop the rocket leaves if they are very large. Preheat the grill to medium.

3. Place the bread under the preheated grill and toast on both sides.

4. Thickly spread the bread with the bean purée. Pile the rocket on top, followed by the tomato quarters. Sprinkle with sea salt and pepper, drizzle with a little oil and serve immediately.

variation

Replace the baby plum tomatoes with sun-dried tomatoes.

cals: 464   fat: 20.1g   sat fat: 2.3g   fibre: 5.7g   carbs: 58.2g   sugar: 2.4g   salt: 4g   protein: 13.3g

roasted vegetable pizzas

prep: 50-55 mins, plus rising and cooling
cook: 30 mins

500 g/1 lb 2 oz plum tomatoes, halved

1 red onion, cut into 8 wedges

1 aubergine, halved and sliced

1 red pepper, quartered and deseeded

1 orange pepper, quartered and deseeded

2 small courgettes, sliced

3 tbsp virgin olive oil, plus extra to serve

15 g/½ oz fresh basil leaves, plus extra to garnish

2 tsp aged balsamic vinegar

175 g/6 oz vegetarian goat's cheese, crumbled

salt and pepper

pizza bases

250 g/9 oz wholemeal plain flour, plus extra to dust

½ tsp sea salt

1 tsp dark muscovado sugar

1 tsp easy-blend dried yeast

1 tbsp virgin olive oil

150–175 ml/5–6 fl oz warm water

1. Preheat the oven to 220°C/425°F/Gas Mark 7. To make the pizza bases, put the flour, salt, sugar and yeast in a mixing bowl and stir. Add the oil, then gradually mix in enough warm water to make a soft but not sticky dough.

2. Lightly dust a work surface with flour. Knead the dough on the surface for 5 minutes, until smooth and elastic. Return it to the bowl, cover with a clean tea-towel and put it in a warm place for 45 minutes, or until doubled in size.

3. Arrange the tomatoes and red onion on a baking sheet in a single layer. Arrange the aubergine and peppers, cut-side down, on a second baking sheet in a single layer. Arrange the courgettes on a third baking sheet in a single layer. Drizzle all the vegetables with a little oil and sprinkle with salt and pepper. Roast for 15 minutes, then take out the courgettes. Roast the other two trays for 5 minutes more. Wrap the peppers in foil and leave to cool, then cut into slices.

4. Remove and discard the tomato skins, if liked, then chop the tomatoes, onion and basil and mix with the vinegar.

5. Lightly flour two baking sheets. Knead the dough, cut it into two pieces and roll out each piece into an oval 30 cm/12 inches long by 15 cm/6 inches wide. Transfer them to the baking sheets, spoon over the tomato mixture, then top with the roasted vegetables. Leave to rise for 15 minutes.

6. Sprinkle the goat's cheese over the pizzas, then bake for 10 minutes, or until the bases are cooked and the cheese has melted. Sprinkle with a little extra oil and basil. Cut each pizza into wedges and serve immediately.

variation

Replace the aubergine with mushrooms for a mushroom and veggie pizza.

serves 4

cals: 625   fat: 31.5g   sat fat: 13g   fibre: 13.7g   carbs: 66.2g   sugar: 13.1g   salt: 2.6g   protein: 25.6g

stilton & mushroom tart

prep: 30 mins, plus chilling and cooling
cook: 35-40 mins

pastry

280 g/10 oz plain flour, plus extra for
    dusting

pinch of salt

1 tbsp fresh chopped thyme, or 1 tsp
    dried thyme

140 g/5 oz butter

3 tbsp cold water

filling

2 tbsp olive oil

3 shallots, finely chopped

15 g/½ oz butter

350 g/12 oz closed-cup mushrooms,
    sliced

140 g/5 oz vegetarian Stilton cheese,
    crumbled

2 tbsp snipped fresh chives

2 large eggs

200 ml/7 fl oz milk

½ tsp grated nutmeg

salt and pepper

mixed salad leaves, to serve (optional)

1. To make the pastry, sift together the flour
and salt into a large bowl, add the thyme
and rub in the butter using your fingertips.
Stir in just enough water to mix to a firm
dough. Wrap in clingfilm and chill in the
refrigerator for about 10 minutes.

2. Preheat the oven to 200°C/400°F/Gas
Mark 6. Roll out the pastry on a lightly floured
surface and use to line a 23-cm/9-inch round,
loose-based flan tin. Line with baking paper
and fill with baking beans, then place on a
baking sheet and bake blind in the preheated
oven for about 10 minutes. Remove the
paper and beans and bake for a further
5 minutes. Reduce the oven temperature to
180°C/350°F/Gas Mark 4.

3. Meanwhile, to make the filling, heat the
oil in a frying pan over a medium heat, add
the shallots and gently fry for 3–4 minutes,
stirring frequently, until soft not brown. Add
the butter, then add the mushrooms and fry,
stirring frequently, until soft and any liquid
has evaporated. Spoon into the pastry case
and top with the cheese and chives.

4. Beat together the eggs, milk, nutmeg,
and salt and pepper to taste, then pour the
mixture over the filling. Bake the tart for
20–25 minutes, or until golden brown and
just set.

5. Remove from the oven and leave to cool
slightly in the tin, then remove from the tin
and serve warm or cold, with a mixed salad,
if liked.

serves 4

cals: 848   fat: 56.1g   sat fat: 31g   fibre: 3.3g   carbs: 62.1g   sugar: 5.3g   salt: 3g   protein: 24.8g

tomato tarte tatin

prep: 25-30 mins, plus resting
cook: 30-35 mins

25 g/1 oz butter

1 tbsp caster sugar

500 g/1 lb 2 oz cherry tomatoes, halved

1 garlic clove, crushed

2 tsp white wine vinegar

salt and pepper

pastry

250 g/9 oz plain flour, sifted

pinch of salt

140 g/5 oz butter

1 tbsp chopped fresh oregano, plus extra to garnish

5–6 tbsp cold water

top tip

Be careful not to over process the pastry – you want it to be soft and not over-worked. Add the water a tablespoon at a time so you can check the consistency.

1. Preheat the oven to 200°C/400°F/Gas Mark 6. Melt the butter in a heavy-based frying pan. Add the sugar and stir over a fairly high heat until just turning golden brown.

2. Remove from the heat and quickly add the tomatoes, garlic and white wine vinegar, stirring to coat evenly. Season with salt and pepper. Tip the tomatoes into a 23-cm/9-inch cake tin, spreading evenly.

3. To make the pastry, place the flour, salt, butter and oregano in a food processor and process until the mixture resembles fine breadcrumbs. Add just enough water to bind to a soft, but not sticky, dough.

4. Roll out the pastry to a 25-cm/10-inch round and place over the tomatoes, tucking in the edges. Pierce with a fork to let out steam.

5. Bake the tart in the preheated oven for 25–30 minutes, until firm and golden. Rest for 2–3 minutes, then run a knife around the edge and turn out onto a warm serving plate. Sprinkle the tarte tatin with chopped oregano and serve warm.

cals: 564   fat: 34.3g   sat fat: 21.3g   fibre: 3.6g   carbs: 57.2g   sugar: 7.3g   salt: 2.2g   protein: 8g

spinach & pine nut frittata

prep: 20 mins
cook: 17-21 mins

250 g/9 oz baby spinach

1 tbsp vegetable oil

25 g/1 oz butter

1 large shallot, halved lengthways and finely sliced

1 garlic clove, thinly sliced

40 g/1½ oz toasted pine nuts

¼ tsp dried red chilli flakes

8 eggs

25 g/1 oz freshly grated vegetarian Parmesan-style cheese

salt and pepper

1. Wash the spinach thoroughly. Drain and put into a saucepan without any extra water. Cover and cook over a medium heat for 5 minutes, stirring occasionally, until just tender. Drain, squeezing out as much liquid as possible, then roughly chop.

2. Heat the oil and butter in a 24-cm/9½-inch non-stick frying pan over a medium heat. Add the shallot and fry for 3 minutes, until translucent. Add the garlic and fry for a further 2 minutes. Stir in the chopped spinach, pine nuts and chilli flakes. Season to taste with salt and pepper.

3. Beat the eggs in a large jug with the cheese. Pour into the pan, stirring to distribute the spinach evenly. Cook over a medium–low heat for 5–7 minutes, until almost set. Meanwhile, preheat the grill to medium.

4. Place the pan under the preheated grill for 1–2 minutes to finish cooking the top of the frittata. Slice into wedges and serve.

serves 4

top tip

Avoid buying spinach with any yellowing leaves. Look for dewy-fresh, dark green leaves.

cals: 348   fat: 27.9g   sat fat: 8.6g   fibre: 2.2g   carbs: 5.8g   sugar: 1.6g   salt: 2.4g   protein: 20g

new inspirations

Nowadays vegetarian food is much more varied than just beans and pasta. Cuisine from other cultures, some of which have a long-standing vegetarian tradition, have inspired restaurants and chefs to cook an exciting selection of vegetarian food.

super snacks & sides

roasted kale crisps

prep: 20 mins
cook: 10–12 mins

250 g/9 oz kale
2 tbsp olive oil
2 pinches of sugar
2 pinches of sea salt
2 tbsp toasted flaked almonds,
  to garnish

1. Preheat the oven to 150°C/300°F/Gas Mark 2. Remove the thick stems and central rib from the kale (leaving about 125 g/ 4½ oz trimmed leaves). Rinse and dry very thoroughly with kitchen paper. Tear into bite-sized pieces and place in a bowl with the oil and sugar, then toss well.

2. Spread about half the kale leaves in a single layer in a large roasting tin, spaced well apart.

3. Sprinkle with a pinch of sea salt and roast on the bottom rack of the preheated oven for 4 minutes.

4. Stir the leaves, then turn the tray so the back is at the front. Roast for a further 1–2 minutes, until the leaves are crisp and very slightly browned at the edges. Repeat with the remaining leaves and sea salt.

5. Sprinkle the kale crisps with the flaked almonds and serve immediately.

top tip

Once they start to crisp, the leaves can quickly burn so check them often.

cals: 122   fat: 9.6g   sat fat: 1.1g   fibre: 1.7g   carbs: 8.1g   sugar: 1.2g   salt: 0.8g   protein: 3g

edamame beans with chilli salt

prep: 15–20 mins
cook: 10–12 mins

2 litres/3½ pints water

300 g/10½ oz edamame beans in pods, stalks removed

salt

sichuan chilli salt

1 tbsp Sichuan peppercorns

1 red chilli, deseeded and very finely diced

5 tbsp sea salt flakes or Himalayan pink crystal salt

variation

To reduce the amount of salt, sprinkle with only 1 teaspoon of chilli salt, and leave out the salt when boiling the beans.

1. Line a tray with kitchen paper. Bring the water to the boil in a large wok or saucepan and add salt to taste.

2. Tip the beans into the boiling water. Bring back to the boil and boil for 3–4 minutes, until the beans are tender-crisp but still bright green. Drain in a colander, then spread out to dry on the prepared tray.

3. Meanwhile, to make the chilli salt, heat a small wok over a high heat. Add the peppercorns and chilli and dry-fry for about 1 minute, stirring, until fragrant and just starting to smoke.

4. Remove from the heat and mix in the salt. Using a large mortar and pestle, roughly crush the mixture until blended.

5. Sprinkle the dry beans with 2 teaspoons of the salt mixture, or extra to taste. (Keep the remainder in a screw-top jar for use in another dish.) Transfer the beans to warmed serving bowls and serve immediately.

cals: 112   fat: 3.6g   sat fat: 0.5g   fibre: 4.1g   carbs: 12.3g   sugar: 3.1g   salt: 3.7g   protein: 9.1g

hummus toasts with olives

prep: 20-25 mins, plus chilling
cook: 5 mins

400 g/14 oz canned chickpeas
juice of 1 large lemon
6 tbsp tahini
2 tbsp olive oil
2 garlic cloves, crushed
salt and pepper
chopped fresh coriander and black
   olives, to garnish

toasts
1 ciabatta loaf, sliced
2 garlic cloves, crushed
1 tbsp chopped fresh coriander
4 tbsp olive oil

1. To make the hummus, first drain the chickpeas, reserving a little of the liquid. Put the chickpeas and liquid in a food processor and blend, gradually adding the lemon juice. Blend well after each addition until smooth.

2. Stir in the tahini and all but 1 teaspoon of the olive oil. Add the garlic, season to taste and blend again until smooth.

3. Spoon the hummus into a serving dish. Drizzle the remaining olive oil over the top and garnish with the chopped coriander and olives. Leave to chill in the refrigerator while preparing the toasts.

4. Preheat the grill. Lay the slices of ciabatta on a grill rack in a single layer. Mix the garlic, coriander and olive oil together and drizzle over the bread slices. Cook under the preheated grill for 2–3 minutes until golden brown, turning once. Serve hot with the hummus.

serves 4

fact

Tahini is a tempting way to eat large quantities of the highly beneficial sesame seed.

cals: 564   fat: 35.8g   sat fat: 4.7g   fibre: 8.1g   carbs: 48.5g   sugar: 1.4g   salt: 2.3g   protein: 13.9g

blue cheese & herb pâté

prep: 20-25 mins, plus chilling
cook: 5 mins

150 g/5½ oz vegetarian low-fat
   soft cheese

350 g/12 oz fromage frais

115 g/4 oz vegetarian blue cheese,
   crumbled

55 g/2 oz dried cranberries,
   finely chopped

5 tbsp chopped fresh herbs, such as
   parsley, chives, dill and tarragon

85 g/3 oz butter

2 tbsp chopped walnuts

granary toast or breadsticks, to serve
   (optional)

1. Beat the soft cheese in a bowl to soften, then gradually beat in the fromage frais until smooth. Add the blue cheese, cranberries and herbs and stir together. Spoon the mixture into 4 x 150-ml/5-fl oz ramekins and carefully smooth the tops.

2. Clarify the butter by gently heating it in a small saucepan until melted. Skim any foam off the surface and discard. Carefully pour the clear yellow top layer into a small jug, discarding the milky liquid left in the pan.

3. Pour a little of the clarified butter over the top of each pâté and sprinkle with the walnuts. Chill for at least 30 minutes until firm. Serve the pâté in the ramekins with granary toast on the side, if liked.

variation

Instead of serving with granary
toast, serve with raw veggies.

cals: 417   fat: 30.7g   sat fat: 17.5g   fibre: 1.4g   carbs: 19.3g   sugar: 14.6g   salt: 1.6g   protein: 18.7g

asparagus with tomato dressing

55 g/2 oz pine nuts

350 g/12 oz tomatoes, peeled, deseeded and chopped

2 tbsp balsamic vinegar

5 tbsp extra virgin olive oil, plus extra for brushing

500 g/1 lb 2 oz young asparagus spears, trimmed

25 g/1 oz vegetarian Parmesan-style cheese, thinly shaved

salt and pepper

1. Brush the grill with oil and preheat. Dry-fry the pine nuts in a heavy-based frying pan for 30–60 seconds, until golden. Tip into a bowl and set aside.

2. Mix together the tomatoes, vinegar and olive oil in a bowl and season with salt and pepper. Set aside.

3. When the grill is hot add the asparagus spears and cook for 3–4 minutes until tender. Carefully transfer to a serving dish. Spoon over the tomato dressing, sprinkle with the pine nuts and cheese shavings and serve immediately.

variation

If you prefer, you can omit the cheese and sprinkle with basil leaves instead.

spicy onion fritters

prep: 20 mins
cook: 40-50 mins

150 g/5½ oz gram flour

1 tsp salt, or to taste

small pinch of bicarbonate of soda

25 g/1 oz ground rice

1 tsp fennel seeds

1 tsp cumin seeds

2 green chillies, finely chopped
(deseeded if you like)

2 large onions (about 400 g/14 oz),
sliced into half-rings and separated

15 g/½ oz fresh coriander, leaves and
stalks, finely chopped

200 ml/7 fl oz cold water

vegetable or groundnut oil,
for deep-frying

top tip

Maintaining a steady temperature is important to ensure that the centres of the fritters are cooked, while the outsides turn brown.

1. Sift the gram flour into a large bowl and add the salt, bicarbonate of soda, ground rice, fennel seeds and cumin seeds. Mix together well, then add the chillies, onions and coriander. Gradually pour in the water and mix until a thick batter is formed and the onions are thoroughly coated with it.

2. Heat enough oil for deep-frying in a large saucepan or deep-fryer to 180–190°C/350–375°F, or until a cube of bread browns in 30 seconds.

3. Add as many small amounts (each about ½ tablespoon) of the batter as will fit in a single layer, without overcrowding the pan. Reduce the heat slightly and cook the fritters for 8–10 minutes, until golden brown and crisp.

4. Use a slotted spoon to remove the fritters from the oil and drain well on kitchen paper. Continue frying until all the batter mixture has been used. Serve hot.

cals: 299   fat: 12.9g   sat fat: 1.3g   fibre: 8.9g   carbs: 38.8g   sugar: 8.9g   salt: 1.9g   protein: 9.2g

feta & spinach parcels

prep: 30 mins, plus cooling
cook: 16-21 mins

2 tbsp olive oil, plus extra for greasing

1 bunch spring onions, chopped

500 g/1 lb 2 oz spinach leaves, roughly chopped

1 egg, beaten

125 g/4½ oz vegetarian feta cheese, crumbled

½ tsp freshly grated nutmeg

6 sheets filo pastry

55 g/2 oz butter, melted

1 tbsp sesame seeds

salt and pepper

top tip

These feta & spinach parcels are perfect for a picnic alongside celery, carrot sticks and a spicy salsa for dipping.

1. Preheat the oven to 200°C/400°F/Gas Mark 6. Grease a baking sheet with oil.

2. Heat the oil in a wok or large frying pan, add the onions and stir-fry for 1–2 minutes. Add the spinach and stir until the leaves are wilted. Cook, stirring occasionally, for 2–3 minutes. Drain off any liquid and leave to cool slightly.

3. Stir the egg, cheese and nutmeg into the spinach and season well.

4. Brush three sheets of pastry with butter. Place another three sheets on top and brush with butter.

5. Cut each sheet down the middle to make six long strips in total. Place a spoonful of the spinach filling on the end of each strip.

6. Lift one corner of pastry over the filling to the opposite side, then turn over the opposite way to enclose. Continue to fold over down the strip to make a triangular parcel, finishing with the seam underneath.

7. Place the parcels on the baking sheet, brush with butter and sprinkle with the sesame seeds. Bake in the preheated oven for 12–15 minutes, or until golden brown and crisp. Serve immediately.

cals: 272   fat: 20.1g   sat fat: 9.2g   fibre: 3g   carbs: 16.1g   sugar: 1.8g   salt: 2.2g   protein: 8.6g

crumbed fennel fritters

prep: 35-40 mins, plus cooling
cook: 45-50 mins

3 fennel bulbs, trimmed

100 g/3½ oz stale white breadcrumbs

100 g/3½ oz vegetarian Parmesan-style
  cheese, finely grated

2 tsp fennel seeds (optional)

1 egg, beaten

sunflower oil, for frying

salt and pepper

lemon wedges, to serve

spiced pepper mayo

2 red peppers

1 egg

1 tsp Dijon mustard

2–3 tbsp white wine vinegar

pinch of salt

300 ml/10 fl oz sunflower oil

2 red chillies, deseeded and chopped

pepper

1. To make the mayo, preheat the oven to 220°C/425°F/Gas Mark 7. Put the red peppers on a baking sheet and cook in the preheated oven, turning frequently, for 10–15 minutes, or until blackened all over.

2. Put the peppers in a polythene bag, seal and leave to cool. Peel off the charred skins and remove the seeds. Chop the peppers.

3. Put the egg, mustard, vinegar and salt into a blender and process to combine. With the motor running, slowly trickle in about one third of the oil. Once the mixture starts to thicken, add the remaining oil more quickly.

4. When all the oil is incorporated, add the chillies and roasted peppers and process until smooth. Stir in a good grinding of pepper, then transfer to a serving dish, cover and refrigerate until required.

5. Bring a large saucepan of lightly salted water to the boil, add the fennel bulbs, bring back to the boil and cook for 15 minutes, or until almost tender. Drain and leave to cool, then carefully slice.

6. Mix the breadcrumbs and cheese together, stir in the fennel seeds, if using, and season to taste with salt and pepper.

7. Transfer the breadcrumb mixture to a large plate. Put the egg in a shallow dish. Coat the fennel slices in the egg and press the breadcrumb mixture firmly on to both sides of each slice.

8. Cover the base of a large frying pan with oil to a depth of about 1 cm/½ inch. Heat over a medium heat, add the fennel slices (in batches if necessary) and cook, turning once, until golden brown.

9. Remove and drain on kitchen paper. Serve immediately with lemon wedges for squeezing over and the mayo on the side.

top tip

When cooking the fritters make sure you don't overcrowd the pan as they won't cook as well.

serves 6

cals: 700   fat: 64.5g   sat fat: 9.3g   fibre: 5.1g   carbs: 21.2g   sugar: 3.1g   salt: 2.1g   protein: 11.6g

vegetarian samosas

prep: 35-45 mins, plus resting
cook: 55-60 mins

250 g/9 oz plain flour

½ tsp salt

40 g/1½ oz ghee or butter, melted, plus extra for greasing

½ tbsp lemon juice

100–125 ml/3½–4 fl oz cold water

vegetable oil, for deep-frying

filling

55 g/2 oz ghee

1 onion, very finely chopped

2 garlic cloves, crushed

1 potato, very finely diced

2 carrots, very finely chopped

2 tsp medium curry powder

1½ tsp ground coriander

1 tsp ground turmeric

1 green chilli, deseeded and finely chopped

1 tsp salt

½ tsp black mustard seeds

300 ml/10 fl oz cold water

100 g/3½ oz frozen peas

55 g/2 oz cauliflower florets, finely chopped

1. To make the filling, melt the ghee in a frying pan over a medium–high heat. Add the onion and garlic and fry for 5 minutes, until soft.

2. Stir in the potato and carrots and continue frying, for 5 minutes. Stir in the curry powder, ground coriander, turmeric, chilli, salt and mustard seeds. Pour in the water and bring to the boil. Reduce the heat to very low and simmer, uncovered, for 15 minutes.

3. Add the peas and cauliflower and continue simmering until the vegetables are tender and the liquid has evaporated. Remove from the heat and set aside.

4. Meanwhile, sift the flour and salt into a bowl. Make a well in the centre, add the ghee and lemon juice and work them into the flour with your fingertips. Gradually add the water until the mixture comes together to form a soft dough. Tip the dough onto a work surface and knead for about 10 minutes, until smooth. Shape into a ball, cover with a damp tea towel and leave to rest for about 15 minutes.

5. Divide the dough into seven equal-sized pieces. Work with one piece at a time and cover the other pieces with a tea towel. On a lightly greased work surface, roll each piece of dough into a 20-cm/8-inch round, then cut in half to make two semi-circles.

6. Working with one semi-circle at a time, wet the edges with water. Place 2 teaspoons of the filling on the dough, just off-centre. Fold one side into the centre, covering the filling. Fold the other side in the opposite direction, overlapping the first fold to form a cone shape. Wet the open edge with more water and press down to seal.

7. Heat enough oil for deep-frying in a large saucepan or deep-fryer until it reaches 180–190°C/350–375°F, or until a cube of bread browns in 30 seconds. Working in batches, deep-fry the samosas, for 2–3 minutes, flipping them over once, until golden brown. Remove with a slotted spoon and drain well on kitchen paper. Serve warm or at room temperature.

top tip

If you don't have ghee use vegetable or groundnut oil to fry the filling instead.

makes 14

cals: 214   fat: 13.9g   sat fat: 5.2g   fibre: 2g   carbs: 19.7g   sugar: 1.7g   salt: 0.7g   protein: 2.9g

preparing vegetables

You don't need to be a fully qualified chef to tackle preparing vegetables. Although some may appear more daunting than others, once you know how, you'll be surprised how easy it is. Wash or scrub everything, but do not leave vegetables soaking in water or their soluble nutrients will leach out. Similarly, do not cut or prepare vegetables too far in advance, as some vitamins, such as vitamin C, diminish once the cut surface is exposed to the air.

How to prepare a pumpkin or squash

1. Cut the pumpkin or squash crossways in half, then spoon the seeds into a bowl and set them aside.

2. Cut the flesh into wedges and peel off the skin.

3. Remove and discard the stringy insides of the flesh using a sharp knife.

4. Cut the pumpkin or squash into 1-cm/½-inch chunks.

5. If wished, the seeds can be roasted at 160°C/325°F/ Gas Mark 3 for 30 minutes. Sprinkle with a little salt before serving.

How to prepare peppers

1. Wash the peppers, then cut lengthways in half.

2. Remove and discard the green stalk.

3. Cut out the white membranes and any remaining seeds, then chop.

How to chop onions

1. Peel the onion and cut in half lengthways.

2. Place the onion halves cut-side down on a chopping board. Cut the onion halves lengthways, taking care not to cut through the root.

3. Turn the blade of the knife so it is parallel with the board and slice the onion, again leaving the root end intact.

4. Grip the onion firmly, then turn the knife again and cut crossways across the original slices until you reach the root end.

How to prepare leeks

1. Remove and discard the root end from the leeks.

2. Trim the opposite end of the leeks, discarding the dark green leaves.

3. Peel off the outer layer of the leeks.

4. Wash the leeks under cold running water to remove any dirt, then slice or chop as required.

sweet potato fries

prep: 15 mins
cook: 15-20 mins

2 sprays of vegetable oil spray
900 g/2 lb sweet potatoes
½ tsp salt
½ tsp ground cumin
¼ tsp cayenne pepper

1. Preheat the oven to 230°C/450°F/Gas Mark 8. Spray a large baking tray with vegetable oil spray.

2. Cut the sweet potatoes into 5-mm/¼-inch thick chips. Arrange them on the prepared baking tray in a single layer and spray them with vegetable oil spray.

3 Mix together the salt, cumin and cayenne pepper in a small bowl, then sprinkle the mixture evenly over the sweet potatoes and toss well.

4. Bake for 15–20 minutes, or until cooked through and lightly coloured. Serve hot.

variation

Use a heaped teaspoon of paprika instead of the cumin and cayenne pepper.

cals: 196   fat: 0.2g   sat fat: trace   fibre: 6.8g   carbs: 45.4g   sugar: 9.4g   salt: 1g   protein: 3.6g

honey-roasted red potatoes

prep: 20 mins
cook: 45-60 mins

vegetable oil spray, for greasing
2 tbsp olive oil
2 tbsp honey
1 tbsp Dijon mustard
½ tsp salt
pinch of cayenne pepper
675 g/1 lb 8 oz small red potatoes,
   halved or quartered
1 shallot, diced
1 garlic clove, finely chopped

1. Preheat the oven to 200°C/400°F/Gas Mark 6 and spray a large baking dish with cooking spray.

2. Put the oil, honey, mustard, salt and cayenne pepper into a small bowl and stir to mix.

3. Put the potatoes, shallot and garlic into the prepared dish and toss together. Drizzle the honey mixture over the top and toss to coat well. Bake in the preheated oven, stirring occasionally, for 45–60 minutes until brown and crisp. Serve hot.

serves 6

cals: 144   fat: 4.8g   sat fat: 0.6g   fibre: 2.1g   carbs: 24.1g   sugar: 7.3g   salt: 0.6g   protein: 2.4g

saucy borlotti beans

prep: 20 mins
cook: 40 mins

600 g/1 lb 5 oz fresh borlotti beans
4 large fresh sage leaves, torn
1 tbsp olive oil
1 large onion, thinly sliced
300 ml/10 fl oz ready-made vegetarian
  tomato sauce
salt and pepper

1. Shell the beans. Bring a large saucepan of water to the boil, add the beans and torn sage leaves, bring back to the boil and simmer for about 12 minutes or until the beans are tender. Drain and set aside.

2. Heat the olive oil in a large, heavy-based frying pan over a medium heat. Add the onion and cook, stirring occasionally, for about 5 minutes until softened and translucent, but not browned. Stir the tomato sauce into the pan with the cooked borlotti beans and the torn sage leaves.

3. Increase the heat and bring to the boil, stirring. Reduce the heat, partially cover and simmer for 10 minutes, or until the sauce has reduced slightly. Adjust the seasoning, transfer to a serving bowl and serve hot.

variation

For a spicy kick, add some chilli powder to the tomato sauce. The beans are also delicious served on top of a jacket potato.

serves 6

cals: 121   fat: 3g   sat fat: 0.3g   fibre: 7.2g   carbs: 18.1g   sugar: 4.7g   salt: 1.4g   protein: 5.8g

roasted broccoli with pine nuts

prep: 25 mins
cook: 18–23 mins

800 g/1 lb 12 oz broccoli, in one piece

6 tbsp olive oil

1 tsp sea salt

¼ tsp pepper

4 tbsp toasted pine nuts

grated rind of ½ lemon

25 g/1 oz vegetarian Parmesan-style cheese shavings

lemon wedges, to garnish

fact

The darker the colour of the broccoli, the more beneficial nutrients it contains. Look for heads rich with colour and avoid any broccoli with pale, yellow or brown patches on the florets.

1. Preheat the oven to 230°C/450°F/Gas Mark 8. Cut off the broccoli crown where it meets the stalk. Remove the outer peel from the stalk. Slice the stalk crossways into 8-cm/3¼-inch pieces, then quarter each slice lengthways. Cut the crown into 4 cm/1½ inch wide wedges.

2. Put the broccoli wedges and stalks in a bowl. Sprinkle with the oil, sea salt and pepper, gently tossing to coat. Spread out in a large roasting tin. Cover tightly with foil and roast on the bottom rack of the preheated oven for 10 minutes.

3. Remove the foil, then roast for a further 5–8 minutes, until just starting to brown. Turn the stalks and wedges over, and roast for a further 3–5 minutes, until tender.

4. Tip into a shallow, warmed serving dish, together with any cooking juices. Sprinkle with the pine nuts and lemon rind, tossing to mix. Scatter the cheese shavings over the top.

5. Garnish with lemon wedges and serve hot, warm or at room temperature.

serves 4

cals: 339   fat: 29.4g   sat fat: 4.4g   fibre: 5.7g   carbs: 15g   sugar: 3.8g   salt: 1.9g   protein: 9.2g

spanish rice

prep: 15 mins
cook: 35 mins

2 tbsp olive oil

½ small onion, chopped

275 g/9¾ oz long-grain white rice

3 garlic cloves, finely chopped

1 tsp ground cumin

1 tsp mild chilli powder

1 tsp dried oregano

600 ml/1 pint vegetable stock

225 ml/8 fl oz ready-made vegetarian tomato sauce

10 g/¼ oz chopped fresh coriander, to garnish (optional)

1. Heat the oil in a large frying pan over a medium heat. Add the onion and cook, stirring frequently, for about 5 minutes until soft. Add the rice and garlic and cook, stirring occasionally, for a further 5 minutes, or until the rice is golden brown.

2. Add the cumin, chilli powder and oregano. Slowly add the stock and tomato sauce, stirring to mix. Bring to the boil, reduce the heat to low, cover and simmer for about 20 minutes until the rice is tender.

3. Remove from the heat, fluff with a fork, garnish with coriander, if using, and serve immediately.

serves 4

cals: 362   fat: 8.8g   sat fat: 1.7g   fibre: 2.5g   carbs: 63.6g   sugar: 5g   salt: 1.9g   protein: 6.5g

steamed greens with coriander

prep: 20 mins
cook: 6 mins

1 head of pointed spring cabbage, weighing about 450 g/1 lb, tough outer leaves discarded

200 g/7 oz baby spinach

large knob of unsalted butter

finely grated rind of ½ lemon

4 tbsp chopped fresh coriander

salt and pepper

1. Cut the cabbage in quarters lengthways and cut out the tough stalk. Slice the quarters crossways into 2-cm/¾-inch ribbons. Steam for 3 minutes, until starting to soften.

2. Arrange the spinach on top of the cabbage, and steam for a further 3 minutes. Drain in a colander to remove any excess liquid.

3. Tip the cabbage and spinach into a warmed serving dish. Stir in the butter, lemon rind and coriander, mixing well.

4. Sprinkle the greens with sea salt and pepper and serve immediately.

serves 4

top tip

Take care not to over steam the greens as they will become soggy.

cals: 70   fat: 3.5g   sat fat: 2g   fibre: 4.2g   carbs: 8.6g   sugar: 0.3g   salt: 1.6g   protein: 3g

brussels sprout & red cabbage slaw

prep: 25 mins, plus standing and cooling
cook: 5 mins

250 g/9 oz Brussels sprouts, tough outer leaves and stalks removed

¼ head of red cabbage, weighing about 225 g/8 oz

½ tsp salt

50 g/1¾ oz pecan nuts

50 g/1¾ oz dried cranberries

6 spring onions, some green included, sliced diagonally

25 g/1 oz fresh flat-leaf parsley leaves

55 g/2 oz salad cress or radish sprouts

dressing

2 tsp clear honey

1½ tsp lemon juice

¼ tsp Dijon mustard

4 tbsp cold-pressed rapeseed oil or walnut oil

1. Cut the Brussels sprouts into quarters, discard the cores and slice the leaves crossways into thin shreds.

2. Remove the outer leaves and core of the red cabbage. Slice lengthways into three segments, then slice the segments crossways into thin shreds.

3. Put the shredded sprouts and cabbage in a serving bowl and sprinkle with the salt. Toss with your hands, then set aside for 30 minutes to soften slightly.

4. Meanwhile, preheat the oven to 150°C/300°F/Gas Mark 2. Put the pecans on a baking tray and toast in the preheated oven for 5 minutes. Leave to cool, then slice in half.

5. Add the pecans, cranberries, spring onions and parsley to the Brussels sprouts and cabbage, gently tossing to mix.

6. To make the dressing, whisk together all the ingredients in a jug. Pour over the salad and gently toss. Scatter the cress over the top. Leave to stand at room temperature for 30 minutes before serving to allow the flavours to develop.

baked celery with cream

prep: 20-25 mins
cook: 40 mins

1 head of celery

½ tsp ground cumin

½ tsp ground coriander

1 garlic clove, crushed

1 red onion, thinly sliced

50 g/1¾ oz pecan nuts, halved

150 ml/5 fl oz vegetable stock

150 ml/5 fl oz single cream

50 g/1¾ oz fresh wholemeal
   breadcrumbs

25 g/1 oz freshly grated vegetarian
   Parmesan-style cheese

salt and pepper

variation

Lightly chopped walnuts make a great alternative to the pecans in this recipe. You can also vary the cheese you use on the top, try vegetarian blue cheese.

1. Preheat the oven to 200°C/400°F/Gas Mark 6. Trim the celery and cut into matchsticks. Place the celery in an ovenproof dish with the cumin, coriander, garlic, red onion and pecan nuts.

2. Mix the stock and cream together in a jug and pour over the vegetables. Season to taste with salt and pepper. Mix the breadcrumbs and cheese together in a small bowl and sprinkle over the top to cover the vegetables.

3. Cook in the preheated oven for 40 minutes, or until the vegetables are tender and the top is crispy. Serve immediately.

cals: 255   fat: 18.6g   sat fat: 6.3g   fibre: 4.8g   carbs: 17.3g   sugar: 5.7g   salt: 2.5g   protein: 7.1g

share it

Having non-vegetarian friends for dinner and not sure what to cook? It needn't be difficult, as long as a meal is varied and balanced most people will be happy to eat vegetarian dishes — and may not even notice.

store it

To ensure that you always have a few staple ingredients to hand, start to build up a storecupboard of useful ingredients, including pasta, rice, spices, canned tomatoes and canned beans.

the main event

risotto primavera

prep: 25 mins
cook: 45-50 mins

1.2 litres/2 pints vegetable stock

1 tbsp olive oil

1 large leek, thinly sliced, white and green slices kept separate

2 garlic cloves, finely chopped

250 g/9 oz short-grain brown rice

150 g/5½ oz baby carrots, tops trimmed, halved lengthways

100 g/3½ oz asparagus spears, woody stems removed

225 g/8 oz courgettes, cut into cubes

25 g/1 oz butter

70 g/2 ½ oz vegetarian Parmesan-style cheese, finely grated

60 g/2¼ oz mixed baby spinach, watercress and rocket leaves

1. Bring the stock to the boil in a saucepan. Meanwhile, heat the oil in a large frying pan over a medium heat. Add the white leek slices and garlic and cook for 3–4 minutes, or until softened but not browned.

2. Stir in the rice and cook for 1 minute. Pour in half the hot stock, bring back to the boil, then cover and simmer for 15 minutes.

3. Stir the rice, then add the carrots and half of the remaining stock and stir again. Cover and cook for 15 minutes.

4. Add the green leek slices, asparagus and courgettes to the rice, then add a little extra stock. Re-cover and cook for 5-6 minutes, or until the vegetables and rice are just tender.

5. Remove from the heat, stir in the butter and two-thirds of the cheese, and add a little more stock if needed. Top with the mixed leaves, cover with the lid, and warm through for 1–2 minutes or until the leaves are just beginning to wilt.

6. Spoon into shallow bowls, sprinkle with the remaining cheese and serve immediately.

cals: 432   fat: 16.9g   sat fat: 8.1g   fibre: 5g   carbs: 59.5g   sugar: 5.3g   salt: 3.7g   protein: 13.6g

four cheese macaroni

prep: 25 mins, plus standing
cook: 35-40 mins

85 g/3 oz freshly grated
vegetarian Parmesan-style cheese

55 g/2 oz fine dry breadcrumbs

400 g/14 oz dried macaroni

40 g/1½ oz butter, plus extra
for greasing

40 g/1½ oz plain flour

450 ml/15 fl oz lukewarm milk

freshly grated nutmeg, to taste

85 g/3 oz vegetarian dolcelatte cheese,
finely chopped

85 g/3 oz vegetarian brie, finely chopped

55 g/2 oz vegetarian mozzarella cheese,
diced

olive oil, for drizzling

salt and pepper

1. Preheat the oven to 200°C/400°F/Gas Mark 6. Lightly grease a large baking dish with butter, then set aside. Mix a third of the Parmesan-style cheese with the breadcrumbs and set aside.

2. Bring a large saucepan of lightly salted water to the boil, add the macaroni, bring back to the boil and cook for 2 minutes less than specified in the packet instructions. Drain well, rinse with cold water, drain again and set aside.

3. Meanwhile, melt the butter in a saucepan over a medium heat. Sprinkle over the flour and stir for 2 minutes, until blended. Remove the pan from the heat and stir in the milk, stirring constantly to prevent lumps forming.

4. Return the pan to the heat, stir in the nutmeg and season to taste with salt and pepper. Slowly bring to the boil, stirring, until the sauce thickens. Stir in the remaining Parmesan-style cheese, the dolcelatte cheese and the brie and continue stirring until the cheese melts and is blended. Stir in the mozzarella cheese.

5. Add the macaroni and stir to coat in the sauce. Adjust the seasoning, if necessary. Tip the mixture into the prepared dish and smooth the surface. Sprinkle the breadcrumb mixture over the top and drizzle with oil.

6. Place the dish on a baking sheet and bake in the preheated oven for 20–25 minutes, until golden brown on top. Leave to stand for a few minutes, then serve straight from the dish.

cals: 922   fat: 40g   sat fat: 22.4g   fibre: 4.2g   carbs: 99.6g   sugar: 9.7g   salt: 3.5g   protein: 38.4g

kale, lemon & chive linguine

prep: 15–20 mins
cook: 20 mins

250 g/9 oz kale, thick stems removed, leaves sliced crossways into thin ribbons

225 g/8 oz dried linguine

8 tbsp olive oil

1 onion, chopped

1 garlic clove, very thinly sliced

grated rind of 1 large lemon

large pinch of dried red chilli flakes

3 tbsp snipped fresh chives

4 tbsp freshly grated vegetarian Parmesan-style cheese

salt and pepper

variation

You don't have to use linguine for this recipe. Smaller pasta shapes such as penne, fusilli or farfalle (bow-tie pasta) would work equally as well.

1. Bring a large saucepan of water to the boil. Add the kale and blanch for 2 minutes, until just wilted. Drain, reserving the water, and set aside.

2. Return the reserved water to the pan and bring to the boil. Add the linguine and cook for 10–12 minutes, until tender but still firm to the bite.

3. Meanwhile, heat the oil in a large frying pan over a medium–high heat. Add the onion and fry for 2–3 minutes, until translucent. Add the garlic and fry for a further minute.

4. Stir in the kale, lemon rind and chilli flakes and season to taste with salt and pepper. Cook over a medium heat for 4–5 minutes, stirring occasionally, until tender but still bright green. Add a little of the cooking water if the mixture becomes dry.

5. Drain the pasta and tip into a warmed serving dish. Add the kale mixture, tossing with the pasta to mix. Stir in the chives and cheese with salt and pepper to taste. Toss again and serve immediately.

serves 3

cals: 693   fat: 39.7g   sat fat: 6.4g   fibre: 6.7g   carbs: 70.6g   sugar: 5g   salt: 2.3g   protein: 15.9g

halloumi & cherry tomato penne

prep: 20 mins
cook: 15 mins

400 g/14 oz dried penne

2 tbsp olive oil

1 red onion, thinly sliced

1 garlic clove, finely chopped

250 g/9 oz cherry plum tomatoes, halved lengthways

250 g/9 oz halloumi cheese, cut into 1-cm/½-inch cubes

3 tbsp chopped fresh basil

salt and pepper

1. Bring a large saucepan of lightly salted water to the boil. Add the pasta, bring back to the boil and cook for 10 minutes until tender but still firm to the bite.

2. Meanwhile, heat the oil in a large frying pan, add the onion and garlic and gently fry, stirring occasionally, for 5–6 minutes, until soft but not brown.

3. Add the tomatoes and cook over a fairly high heat, shaking the pan occasionally, for 2–3 minutes, or until soft. Remove from the pan, set aside and keep warm.

4. Add the halloumi to the pan and fry over a medium heat, stirring, for 2–3 minutes, or until golden brown. Return the tomato mixture to the pan with the basil and season to taste with salt and pepper.

5. Drain the pasta, then add to the pan and toss with the tomato mixture until evenly combined. Serve immediately.

3

4

5

serves 4

cals: 659   fat: 23.6g   sat fat: 11.2g   fibre: 4.8g   carbs: 82.8g   sugar: 6.9g   salt: 2g   protein: 28.1g

vegetable chilli

prep: 25 mins
cook: 1½ hours

1 aubergine, cut into 2.5-cm/1-inch slices

1 tbsp olive oil, plus extra for brushing

1 large red onion, finely chopped

2 red or yellow peppers, deseeded and finely chopped

3–4 garlic cloves, finely chopped or crushed

800 g/1 lb 12 oz canned chopped tomatoes

1 tbsp mild chilli powder

½ tsp ground cumin

½ tsp dried oregano

2 small courgettes, quartered lengthways and sliced

400 g/14 oz canned kidney beans, drained and rinsed

450 ml/15 fl oz water

1 tbsp tomato purée

6 spring onions, finely chopped

115 g/4 oz vegetarian Cheddar cheese, grated

salt and pepper

1. Brush the aubergine slices on one side with olive oil. Heat half the oil in a large, heavy-based frying pan over a medium–high heat. Add the aubergine slices, oiled-side up, and cook for 5–6 minutes, or until browned on one side. Turn the slices over, cook on the other side until browned and transfer to a plate. Cut into bite-sized pieces.

2. Heat the remaining oil in a large saucepan over a medium heat. Add the onion and peppers and cook, stirring occasionally, for 3–4 minutes, or until the onion is just softened, but not browned.

3. Add the garlic and cook for a further 2–3 minutes, or until the onion is beginning to colour. Add the tomatoes, chilli powder, cumin and oregano. Season to taste with salt and pepper. Bring just to the boil, reduce the heat, cover and simmer gently for 15 minutes.

4. Add the courgettes, aubergine pieces and kidney beans. Stir in the water and the tomato purée. Return to the boil, then cover and continue simmering for 45 minutes, or until the vegetables are tender. Taste and adjust the seasoning if necessary. Ladle into serving bowls and top with spring onions and cheese.

cals: 364   fat: 17g   sat fat: 6.8g   fibre: 13.7g   carbs: 37.8g   sugar: 17g   salt: 2g   protein: 17.9g

ratatouille

prep: 20–25 mins
cook: 1 hour 5 mins

150 ml/5 fl oz olive oil

2 onions, sliced

2 garlic cloves, finely chopped

2 medium-sized aubergines, roughly chopped

4 courgettes, roughly chopped

2 yellow peppers, deseeded and chopped

2 red peppers, deseeded and chopped

1 bouquet garni

3 large tomatoes, peeled, deseeded and roughly chopped

salt and pepper

1. Heat the oil in a large saucepan. Add the onions and cook over a low heat, stirring occasionally, for 5 minutes, or until softened. Add the garlic and cook, stirring frequently for a further 2 minutes. Add the aubergines, courgettes and peppers. Increase the heat to medium and cook, stirring occasionally, until the peppers begin to colour. Add the bouquet garni, reduce the heat, cover and simmer gently for 40 minutes.

2. Stir in the chopped tomatoes and season to taste with salt and pepper. Re-cover the saucepan and simmer gently for a further 10 minutes. Remove and discard the bouquet garni. Serve warm.

top tip

This dish is also delicious served cold. Pack up leftovers for lunch or take to a barbecue or picnic.

serves 4

cals: 489   fat: 40.7g   sat fat: 5.4g   fibre: 13.7g   carbs: 34.4g   sugar: 18.3g   salt: 1.5g   protein: 6.3g

marinated tofu with wild rice

prep: 20 mins, plus marinating
cook: 45 mins

400 g/14 oz firm tofu, drained
1 tbsp chopped fresh thyme
finely grated rind of 1 lemon
1 tsp crushed dried chillies
3 tbsp extra virgin olive oil
300 g/10½ oz wild rice
6 spring onions, sliced diagonally
salt and pepper

top tip

Wild rice takes about 45 minutes to cook. To reduce the cooking time, place in a bowl, cover with boiling water and leave to stand for 4 hours. Drain and cook in boiling water for 20 minutes.

1. Place the tofu on a clean tea towel and lightly press to remove as much excess moisture as possible. Cut the tofu into 2-cm/¾-inch thick strips and place in a non-metallic dish.

2. Mix the thyme, lemon rind and chillies with about half the oil and spread over the tofu, gently turning to coat evenly. Cover with clingfilm and leave to marinate in the refrigerator for about 1 hour, or overnight.

3. Cook the rice according to the packet instructions. Drain well.

4. Meanwhile, heat the remaining oil in a wok or large frying pan, add the spring onions and stir-fry for 30 seconds. Remove and reserve the spring onions, add the tofu to the pan and cook for a further 4–5 minutes, turning occasionally, until golden brown.

5. Season to taste with salt and pepper and serve the tofu and reserved spring onions on top of the rice.

cals: 432   fat: 13.8g   sat fat: 1.9g   fibre: 5.9g   carbs: 61.2g   sugar: 3.8g   salt: 1.6g   protein: 18.5g

french bean casserole

prep: 15 mins
cook: 45-50 mins

500 g/1 lb 2 oz French beans, cut into
   4-cm/1½ -inch lengths

300 ml/10 fl oz canned condensed
   mushroom soup

225 ml/8 fl oz milk

1 tsp soy sauce

1 tbsp corn oil

15 g/½ oz butter

1 onion, sliced into rings

salt

1. Preheat the oven to 180°C/350°F/Gas
Mark 4. Bring a saucepan of lightly salted
water to the boil and add the beans. Bring
back to the boil and cook for 5 minutes.
Drain well.

2. Put the soup, milk and soy sauce into a
bowl and mix together, then stir in the beans.
Tip into a 1.5-litre/2½-pint casserole and
distribute evenly. Bake in the preheated oven
for 25–30 minutes, until bubbling and golden.

3. Meanwhile, heat the oil and butter in a
frying pan, add the onion rings and fry over
a fairly high heat, stirring frequently, until
golden brown and crisp. Remove and drain on
kitchen paper.

4. Arrange the onion rings on top of the
casserole and bake for a further 5 minutes.
Serve hot.

serves 4

fact

French beans have a high protein content that is essential for healthy skin, bones and muscles.

cals: 213   fat: 13.7g   sat fat: 3.9g   fibre: 4.1g   carbs: 19.5g   sugar: 9.2g   salt: 1.8g   protein: 5.4g

potato & lemon casserole

prep: 20 mins
cook: 30-40 mins

100 ml/3½ fl oz olive oil
2 red onions, cut into 8 wedges
3 garlic cloves, crushed
2 tsp ground cumin
2 tsp ground coriander
pinch of cayenne pepper
1 carrot, thickly sliced
2 small turnips, quartered
1 courgette, sliced
500 g/1 lb 2 oz potatoes, thickly sliced
grated rind and juice of 2 large lemons
300 ml/10 fl oz vegetable stock
2 tbsp chopped fresh coriander
salt and pepper

1. Heat the olive oil in a flameproof casserole. Add the onions and sauté over a medium heat, stirring frequently, for 3 minutes.

2. Add the garlic and cook for 30 seconds. Stir in the ground cumin, ground coriander and cayenne and cook, stirring constantly, for 1 minute.

3. Add the carrot, turnips, courgette and potatoes and stir to coat in the oil.

4. Add the lemon juice and rind and the stock. Season to taste with salt and pepper. Cover and cook over a medium heat, stirring occasionally, for 20–30 minutes until tender.

5. Remove the lid, sprinkle in the chopped fresh coriander and stir well. Serve immediately.

variation

Try swapping the turnips for a similar weight of butternut squash, peeled and cubed.

serves 4

cals: 382   fat: 26.4g   sat fat: 3.8g   fibre: 7.1g   carbs: 35.7g   sugar: 8.6g   salt: 2.3g   protein: 4.4g

vegetable stock

Making your own vegetable stock sounds difficult and time consuming but in reality it's surprisingly easy! The ingredients are inexpensive and widely available, and very little hands-on cooking time is needed.

You can substitute other vegetables if you particularly dislike one, or if you have other ingredients to hand that you want to use. Make a large batch and store in the freezer for up to 3 months – it is best to do this in portions so you only use what you need.

Perfect for using in soups, stews, casseroles and risottos this stock is both delicious and versatile.

top tip

Don't season this stock with salt, when the stock concentrates it can become too salty.

basic vegetable stock

prep: 20 mins, plus cooling
cook: 1¼ hours

2 tbsp sunflower oil

1 onion, finely chopped

2 leeks, thinly sliced

2 celery sticks, finely chopped

1 large potato, diced

2 carrots, thinly sliced

2 small parsnips, thinly sliced

1 small turnip, thinly sliced

2 bay leaves

6 fresh parsley sprigs

150 ml/5 fl oz vegetarian dry white
   wine

1 litre/1¾ pints water

1. Heat the oil in a large saucepan. Add the onion, leeks, celery and potato and cook over a low heat, stirring frequently, for about 8 minutes, until the vegetables have softened and just beginning to colour.

2. Add the carrots, parsnips, turnip, bay leaves, parsley sprigs and white wine, stir well and cook for 2 minutes, until the alcohol has evaporated. Increase the heat to medium, pour in the water and bring to the boil. Reduce the heat, cover and simmer for 1 hour.

3. Remove the pan from the heat and strain the stock into a bowl through a fine sieve, pressing the vegetables with the back of a ladle to extract as much liquid as possible; do not press the vegetables through the sieve.

4. Strain again and leave to cool completely, then cover with clingfilm and store in the refrigerator for up to 2 days. Alternatively, freeze for up to 3 months.

Makes 1 litre/1¾ pints

greens, pea & bean burgers

prep: 25-30 mins, plus standing
cook: 15-17 mins

115 g/4 oz peppery salad leaves, such as rocket, mustard greens, pak choi (green part only) or a mixture, thick stems removed

60 g/2¼ oz cooked peas, mashed

400 g/14 oz canned butter beans, drained, rinsed and mashed

1 tbsp grated onion

1½ tbsp chopped fresh mint

¼ tsp salt

pinch of pepper

1 egg, beaten

40 g/1½ oz stale breadcrumbs

3 tbsp vegetable oil

to serve (optional)

4 oval pittas, halved crossways

cherry tomatoes, halved

mayonnaise

1. Roughly slice the salad leaves. Steam for 3 minutes, then drain and rinse under cold running water, squeezing out as much liquid as possible.

2. Combine the cooked greens with the peas, beans, onion, mint, salt, pepper and egg. Mix thoroughly with a fork. Stir in the breadcrumbs, mixing well. Leave to stand at room temperature for 30 minutes.

3. Divide the mixture into 8 x 1-cm/½-inch thick patties, each 6 cm/2½ inches in diameter, firming the edges well.

4. Heat the oil in a non-stick frying pan over a medium–high heat. Working in batches, add the patties and fry for 2½–3 minutes on each side, turning carefully, until golden and crisp. Meanwhile, preheat the grill to medium.

5. If liked, toast the pitta halves under the preheated grill. Stuff each half with a bean patty, cherry tomato halves and a dollop of mayonnaise. Serve immediately.

cals: 118   fat: 6.3g   sat fat: 0.8g   fibre: 2.7g   carbs: 10g   sugar: 1.1g   salt: 0.3g   protein: 4.6g

tacos with chickpea salsa

prep: 20-25 mins
cook: 6-7 mins

2 firm, ripe avocados
1 tbsp lime juice
1 tomato, diced
1 tbsp olive oil
1 small onion, sliced
400 g/14 oz canned chickpeas, drained
1 tsp mild chilli powder
8 Cos lettuce leaves
8 small corn tortillas
2 tbsp chopped fresh coriander, plus
    extra sprigs to garnish
salt and pepper
soured cream, to serve (optional)

1. Halve, stone, peel and dice the avocados and toss with the lime juice. Stir in the tomato and season well with salt and pepper.

2. Heat the oil in a saucepan and fry the onion for 3–4 minutes, or until golden brown. Mash the chickpeas with a fork and stir into the pan with the chilli powder. Heat gently, stirring, for 2 minutes.

3. Divide the lettuce between the tortillas. Stir the chopped coriander into the avocado and tomato mixture, then spoon into the tortillas.

4. Add a spoonful of the chickpea mixture to each tortilla and top with a spoonful of soured cream, if liked. Garnish with coriander sprigs and serve immediately.

fact

Chickpeas are a great protein food for vegetarians and a very good source of fibre.

cals: 401   fat: 25.7g   sat fat: 3.3g   fibre: 13g   carbs: 37.2g   sugar: 3.8g   salt: 1.5g   protein: 9.1g

tandoori mushroom curry

prep: 15–20 mins
cook: 40 mins

2 tbsp vegetable or groundnut oil

1 tsp cumin seeds

1 tsp coriander seeds

1 onion, finely chopped

2 tsp ground coriander

1 tsp ground cumin

6 black peppercorns

½ tsp freshly ground cardamom seeds

1 tsp ground turmeric

1 tbsp tandoori masala

1 red chilli, finely chopped

2 garlic cloves, crushed

2 tsp grated fresh ginger

800 g/1 lb 12 oz canned chopped
    tomatoes

600 g/1 lb 5 oz chestnut or button
    mushrooms, halved or thickly sliced

2 tsp salt

200 g/7 oz fresh or frozen peas

4 tbsp roughly chopped fresh coriander

6 tbsp single cream

1. Heat the oil in a large saucepan over a medium heat. Add the cumin seeds and coriander seeds and cook for 1 minute, or until sizzling.

2. Add the onion, ground coriander, cumin, peppercorns, ground cardamom seeds, turmeric, tandoori masala, chilli, garlic and ginger. Cook, stirring, for 2–3 minutes, or until onion is soft and the mixture is aromatic.

3. Add the tomatoes, mushrooms and salt. Stir until well combined. Bring to the boil, then reduce the heat to low and cook, uncovered, for 25 minutes.

4. Add the peas and stir to mix well. Cook for a further 4–5 minutes, or until piping hot. Remove from the heat, scatter over the coriander and drizzle over the cream. Stir to mix well. Serve immediately.

cals: 224   fat: 13.2g   sat fat: 3.5g   fibre: 5g   carbs: 22.9g   sugar: 11.7g   salt: 3.2g   protein: 8.9g

roasted peppers

prep: 20 mins, plus cooling and marinating
cook: 40 mins

2 red peppers, halved and deseeded

2 yellow peppers, halved and deseeded

1 red onion, roughly chopped

2 garlic cloves, finely chopped

6 tbsp olive oil

100 g/3½ oz vegetarian mini mozzarella cheese pearls, drained

2 tbsp roughly torn fresh basil

2 tbsp balsamic vinegar

salt and pepper

top tip

This is a light and fresh summer evening meal. In the winter, try serving hot with a side of rice, pasta or couscous. Both ways are equally wonderful!

1. Preheat the oven to 190°C/375°F/Gas Mark 5. Put the peppers cut side up in a shallow roasting tin. Scatter over the onion and garlic, season well with salt and pepper and drizzle over 3 tablespoons of the olive oil. Roast for 40 minutes, or until the peppers are tender. Leave to cool.

2. Arrange the cold peppers in a serving dish and pour over any juices left in the roasting tin. Scatter over the mozzarella and basil.

3. To make the dressing, whisk together the remaining olive oil and the balsamic vinegar, then drizzle over the peppers. Cover and leave to marinate in the refrigerator for at least 2 hours before serving.

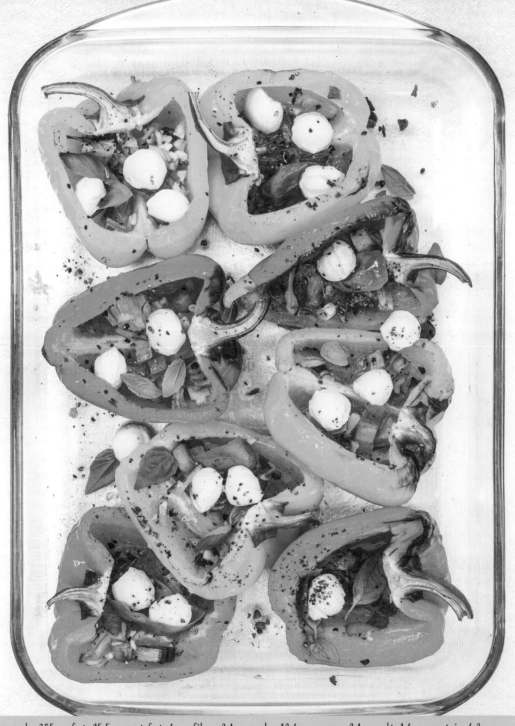

cals: 305   fat: 25.5g   sat fat: 6g   fibre: 3.4g   carbs: 13.6g   sugar: 8.4g   salt: 1.6g   protein: 6.3g

roasted pumpkin & walnut pesto

1 kg/2 lb 4 oz pumpkin, deseeded, peeled and cut into 2-cm/¾-inch slices

2 tbsp virgin olive oil

500 g/1 lb 2 oz fresh wholewheat tagliatelle

salt and pepper

walnut pesto

85 g/3 oz walnuts, broken into pieces

6 tbsp virgin olive oil

15 g/½ oz fresh basil

25 g/1 oz vegetarian Parmesan-style cheese, thinly shaved, plus extra to serve (optional)

70 g/2½ oz rocket leaves

1. Preheat the oven to 200°C/400°F/Gas Mark 6. Arrange the pumpkin on a large baking sheet in a single layer. Drizzle with the oil and season with salt and pepper. Roast for 20–25 minutes, or until just tender.

2. Meanwhile, to make the pesto, put the walnuts in a large frying pan and toast for 2–3 minutes, or until just beginning to brown. Transfer to a food processor or blender, pour in the oil and process until coarsely ground. Add the basil, cheese and half the rocket leaves and process again until you have a coarse pesto.

3. Bring a large saucepan of water to the boil, add the tagliatelle and cook for 3–4 minutes, or according to the packet instructions, until al dente.

4. Drain the pasta and pour a little of the cooking water into a jug. Return the pasta to the pan. Cut the pumpkin into cubes and add this to the pasta. Drizzle over the pesto and gently toss together, adding a little of the reserved pasta water if needed to loosen the sauce. Top with the remaining rocket. Spoon into bowls and serve with extra cheese, if liked.

variation

Butternut squash instead of
pumpkin works equally well in
this recipe.

cals: 715   fat: 46g   sat fat: 7g   fibre: 10.6g   carbs: 66g   sugar: 6.7g   salt: 2.1g   protein: 17.3g

spicy vegetable & tofu udon noodles

prep: 20 mins
cook: 12-15 mins

225 g/8 oz French beans, topped and tailed and cut into 2.5-cm/1-inch pieces

2 tbsp water

2 tbsp sriracha

2 tbsp rice vinegar

2 tbsp soy sauce

350 g/12 oz dried udon noodles

1 tbsp vegetable oil

1 tbsp sesame oil

2½ garlic cloves, finely chopped

225 g/8 oz extra firm tofu, cut into 2.5-cm/1-inch cubes

225 g/8 oz baby spinach

2 tbsp toasted sesame seeds, to garnish

1. Place the beans in a microwave-safe bowl with the water. Cover and microwave on high for 2 minutes, then drain. Stir together the sriracha, vinegar and soy sauce in a bowl. Cook the noodles according to the packet instructions. Drain and set aside.

2. Meanwhile, heat the vegetable oil and sesame oil in a large frying pan over a medium–high heat. Add the garlic and cook, stirring, for 1 minute. Add the tofu and beans and cook, stirring occasionally, for 1 minute, until the beans are tender and the tofu is beginning to brown.

3. Stir in the spinach and cook for 2 minutes, until it wilts. Add the noodles and sauce mixture and toss to combine. Serve garnished with toasted sesame seeds.

top tip

If you don't have sriracha,
substitute chilli-garlic paste.

cals: 472   fat: 11.3g   sat fat: 1.4g   fibre: 7.2g   carbs: 76.2g   sugar: 4.2g   salt: 2.5g   protein: 17g

butternut squash stir-fry

prep: 20 mins
cook: 20–25 mins

1 kg/2 lb 4 oz butternut squash, peeled
and deseeded
3 tbsp groundnut oil
1 onion, sliced
2 cloves garlic, crushed
1 tsp coriander seeds
1 tsp cumin seeds
2 tbsp chopped fresh coriander
150 ml/5 fl oz coconut milk
100 ml/3½ fl oz water
100 g/3½ oz salted cashew nuts

to garnish (optional)
freshly grated lime rind
fresh coriander
lime slices

1. Slice the squash into small, bite-sized cubes, using a sharp knife. Heat the groundnut oil in a large, preheated wok. Add the butternut squash, the onion and the garlic to the wok and stir-fry for 5 minutes.

2. Stir in the coriander seeds, cumin seeds and chopped coriander, and stir-fry for 1 minute.

3. Add the coconut milk and water to the wok and bring to the boil. Cover the wok and leave to simmer for 10–15 minutes, or until the squash is tender. Add the cashew nuts and stir to combine thoroughly.

4. Transfer to warmed serving dishes and garnish with the lime rind, the coriander and the lime slices, if liked. Serve immediately.

variation

Add 2 fresh, finely chopped chillies to the stir-fry with the onion and garlic.

cals: 443   fat: 30.4g   sat fat: 11.2g   fibre: 6.9g   carbs: 43.3g   sugar: 9.3g   salt: 0.4g   protein: 8g

little helpers

Children love to help out in the kitchen and baking is a great way of encouraging any budding chefs! Ask children to help with weighing and mixing ingredients or lining tins with paper cases – and, of course, decorating at the end!

something sweet →

mango & ginger sundaes

prep: 20 mins
cook: 8–10 mins

1 large, ripe mango
115 g/4 oz ginger biscuits
1 litre/1¾ pints vanilla ice cream
2 tbsp roughly chopped almonds, toasted

butterscotch sauce

100 g/3½ oz light muscovado sugar
100 g/3½ oz golden syrup
55 g/2 oz unsalted butter
100 ml/3½ fl oz double cream
½ tsp vanilla extract

1. To make the butterscotch sauce, melt the sugar, golden syrup and butter in a small pan and simmer for 3 minutes, stirring, until smooth. Stir in the cream and vanilla extract, then remove from the heat.

2. Peel and stone the mango and cut into 1-cm/½-inch cubes. Place the ginger biscuits in a polythene bag and crush lightly with a rolling pin.

3. Place half the mango in four sundae dishes and top each with a scoop of the ice cream. Spoon over a little butterscotch sauce and sprinkle with crushed biscuits. Repeat with the remaining ingredients.

4. Sprinkle some of the almonds over the top of each sundae and serve immediately.

top tip

Add some grated white chocolate
to the top of each sundae for an
extra-special treat.

baked lemon cheesecake

prep: 25 mins, plus chilling and cooling
cook: 45-50 mins

55 g/2 oz butter, plus extra for greasing
175 g/6 oz gingernut biscuits, crushed
3 lemons
300 g/10½ oz vegetarian ricotta cheese
200 g/7 oz Greek-style yogurt
4 eggs
1 tbsp cornflour
100 g/3½ oz caster sugar
strips of lemon zest, to decorate

1. Preheat the oven to 180°C/350°F/Gas Mark 4. Grease a 20-cm/8-inch round springform cake tin and line with baking paper.

2. Melt the butter in a pan and stir in the biscuit crumbs. Press into the base of the prepared cake tin. Chill until firm.

3. Meanwhile, finely grate the rind and squeeze the juice from the lemons and add to a large bowl. Add the ricotta, yogurt, eggs, cornflour and caster sugar, and whisk until a smooth batter is formed.

4. Carefully spoon the mixture into the tin. Bake in the preheated oven for 40–45 minutes, or until just firm and golden brown.

5. Cool the cheesecake completely in the tin, then run a knife around the edge to loosen and turn out onto a serving plate. Decorate with lemon zest.

top tip

Serve with ice cream or clotted cream for a really indulgent treat.

cals: 353   fat: 19.6g   sat fat: 11.1g   fibre: 0.7g   carbs: 33.7g   sugar: 20.9g   salt: 0.5g   protein: 11.4g

chilli chocolate mousse

prep: 25 mins, plus cooling and setting
cook: 5 mins

150 g/5½ oz 70% plain chocolate,
   broken into pieces

pinch of salt

4 large eggs, separated

55 g/2 oz caster sugar

150 ml/5 fl oz double cream

1 tsp chipotle powder

2 tsp orange zest

100 g/3½ oz sour cherries

100 ml/3½ fl oz dark rum

55 g/2 oz roasted hazelnuts

top tip

For a non-alcoholic version of this recipe omit the rum-soaked cherries and replace with whipped cream. Then top with the hazelnuts and orange zest.

1. Place the chocolate pieces in a large heatproof bowl set over a pan of gently simmering water and heat, stirring occasionally, until melted. Remove from the heat and set aside to cool.

2. Once the chocolate has cooled, beat in the salt, egg yolks and sugar.

3. In a separate bowl whisk the double cream until it has thickened slightly.

4. In a clean bowl whisk the egg whites until stiff peaks have formed.

5. Add the chipotle powder and 1 teaspoon of the orange zest to the chocolate mixture, then fold in the cream, followed by the egg whites. Divide between four glasses and place in the refrigerator for 2 hours to set.

6. Meanwhile, soak the sour cherries in the rum and roughly chop the hazelnuts.

7. Just before serving, remove the mousses from the refrigerator and top with the rum-soaked sour cherries, the hazelnuts and the remaining orange zest.

cals: 683   fat: 47.8g   sat fat: 22.7g   fibre: 5.9g   carbs: 37.9g   sugar: 26.8g   salt: 1g   protein: 12.8g

spiced plum & blackberry brûlées

prep: 25 mins, plus cooling and chilling
cook: 15 mins

300 g/10½ oz plums, stoned and sliced
175 g/6 oz blackberries
2 tbsp water
¼ tsp ground cinnamon
5 tbsp light muscovado sugar
225 ml/8 fl oz double cream
225 g/8 oz Greek-style natural yogurt

1. Put the plums, blackberries and water in a saucepan, sprinkle over the cinnamon and 2 tablespoons of the sugar, then cover and cook over a medium-low heat for 10 minutes, or until just tender. Leave to cool.

2. Put the cream in a large bowl and whisk until soft swirls form, then fold in the yogurt.

3. Spoon the fruit and a little of the juice into 6 x ovenproof 175-ml/6-fl oz ramekins or soufflé dishes. Dot teaspoons of the cream mixture over the top, then spread it into an even layer. Chill for at least 30 minutes.

4. Preheat the grill. Sprinkle the remaining 3 tablespoons of sugar over the tops of the dishes, then stand them in the base of the grill pan, pack ice around them to keep them cold and grill for 4–5 minutes, or until the sugar has dissolved and caramelised. Leave to cool for 2 minutes, then serve.

top tip

Caramelise the sugar at the very last minute with a cook's blowtorch instead of grilling.

cals: 284   fat: 20g   sat fat: 12.5g   fibre: 2.3g   carbs: 23.1g   sugar: 20.9g   salt: trace   protein: 4.7g

berry & oat crumbles

prep: 20-25 mins, plus cooling
cook: 20 mins

450 g/1 lb red plums, halved, stoned
and diced

115 g/4 oz raspberries

25 g/1 oz light muscovado sugar

3 tbsp water

ready-made custard, to serve
(optional)

topping

85 g/3 oz plain flour

20 g/¾ oz porridge oats

20 g/¾ oz barley flakes

40 g/1½ oz light muscovado sugar

40 g/1½ oz unsalted butter,
chilled and diced

1. Preheat the oven to 180°C/350°F/Gas
Mark 4. Put the plums, raspberries, 25 g/
1 oz sugar and the water into a heavy-based
saucepan. Cover and simmer for 5 minutes, or
until the fruit has softened.

2. To make the topping, put the flour, porridge
oats, barley flakes and sugar into a mixing
bowl and stir. Rub in the butter using your
fingertips until the mixture resembles fine
crumbs.

3. Spoon the fruit mixture into 8 x 150-ml/
5-fl oz metal pudding moulds and stand them
on a baking tray. Sprinkle the topping on top.

4. Bake in the preheated oven for 15 minutes,
or until golden. Allow the crumbles to cool for
5–10 minutes, then serve topped with small
spoonfuls of custard, if liked.

cals: 157 fat: 4.6g sat fat: 2.6g fibre: 2.5g carbs: 27.9g sugar: 14.4g salt: trace protein: 2.4g

apple pie

prep: 35–40 mins, plus chilling
cook: 50 mins

175 g/6 oz plain flour

pinch of salt

85 g/3 oz butter, cut into pieces

85 g/3 oz vegetable shortening, cut into small pieces

about 1–2 tbsp water

beaten egg or milk, for glazing

filling

750 g–1 kg/1 lb 10 oz–2 lb 4 oz cooking apples, peeled, cored and sliced

125 g/4½ oz soft light brown sugar, plus extra for sprinkling

½–1 tsp ground cinnamon

top tip

Instead of making leaf shapes out of the remaining pastry, get creative and make something else. Try hearts, stars or apples.

1. Sift the flour and salt into a mixing bowl. Add the butter and vegetable shortening, and rub in with your fingertips until the mixture resembles fine breadcrumbs. Add enough cold water to mix to a firm dough. Wrap in clingfilm and chill for 30 minutes.

2. Preheat the oven to 220°C/425°F/Gas Mark 7. Thinly roll out almost two thirds of the pastry and use to line a deep 23-cm/9-inch pie dish.

3. To make the filling, mix the apples with the sugar and cinnamon, and pack into the pastry case.

4. Roll out the remaining pastry to form a lid. Dampen the edges of the pie rim with water and position the lid, pressing the edges firmly together. Trim and crimp the edges. Use the pastry trimmings to cut out leaves. Dampen and attach to the top of the pie. Glaze the pie with beaten egg, make one or two slits in the top and place the pie on a baking sheet.

5. Bake in the preheated oven for 20 minutes, then reduce the temperature to 180°C/350°F/Gas Mark 4 and bake for a further 30 minutes, or until the pastry is a light golden brown. Sprinkle with sugar and serve hot or cold.

serves 8

cals: 346   fat: 17.3g   sat fat: 8.5g   fibre: 2.2g   carbs: 46.9g   sugar: 27.1g   salt: 0.7g   protein: 3.1g

chocolate fondants with toffee sauce

prep: 30 mins, plus chilling and standing
cook: 20–25 mins

150 g/5½ oz unsalted butter

4 tsp cocoa powder

150 g/5½ oz plain chocolate, roughly chopped

2 eggs, plus 2 egg yolks

125 g/4½ oz caster sugar

25 g/1 oz plain flour

icing sugar, sifted, for dusting (optional)

toffee sauce

55 g/2 oz unsalted butter

55 g/2 oz light muscovado sugar

1 tbsp runny honey

150 ml/5 fl oz double cream

1. Melt 25 g/1 oz of the butter in a small saucepan, then brush it over the insides of 10 x 125-ml/4-fl oz ovenproof ramekins. Sift a little cocoa into each ramekin, then tilt to coat the base and sides evenly, tapping out any excess.

2. Put the chocolate and remaining 125 g/4½ oz butter in a heatproof bowl, set the bowl over a saucepan of gently simmering water and heat until melted, stirring from time to time.

3. Put the eggs, egg yolks and caster sugar into a mixing bowl and whisk together until thick and frothy and the whisk leaves a trail when raised above the mixture. Sift over the flour, then gently fold it in.

4. Fold the melted chocolate mixture into the egg mixture until smooth. Pour it into the prepared ramekins, cover and chill in the fridge for 1 hour, or overnight if time allows.

5. To make the toffee sauce, put the butter, light muscovado sugar and honey into a heavy-based saucepan and heat gently for 3–4 minutes, or until the butter has melted and the sugar dissolved.

6. Boil for a further 1–2 minutes, stirring, until it begins to smell of toffee and thicken. Remove from the heat and stir in the cream.

7. Preheat the oven to 180°C/350°F/Gas Mark 4. Take the ramekins out of the fridge and leave at room temperature for 10 minutes.

8. Bake in the preheated oven for 10–12 minutes, or until well risen, the tops are crusty and the centres still slightly soft. Reheat the sauce over a low heat, if needed.

9. Dust the desserts with sifted icing sugar, if liked. Serve with the sauce in a jug for guests to pour on.

top tip

These chocolate fondants can be prepared in advance then left in the fridge for up to 24 hours.

makes 10

cals: 416   fat: 32.2g   sat fat: 19.4g   fibre: 1.9g   carbs: 29.3g   sugar: 23.6g   salt: trace   protein: 3.9g

melon medley ice pops

prep: 20 mins, plus freezing
cook: no cooking

finely grated rind and juice of 1 lime

100 ml/3½ fl oz sugar syrup

175 g/6 oz deseeded and roughly chopped watermelon flesh

175 g/6 oz deseeded and roughly chopped cantaloupe melon flesh

1. Put the lime juice, lime rind and sugar syrup into a measuring jug and stir together well. Put the watermelon and half the lime syrup in a blender and whizz until smooth. Pour the mixture into 8 x 100-ml/3½-fl oz ice pop moulds. Freeze for 4 hours, or until firm.

2. When the watermelon mixture is frozen, put the cantaloupe melon and the remaining lime syrup in the blender and whizz until smooth. Pour over the frozen watermelon mixture. Insert the ice pop sticks and freeze for 4 hours, or until firm.

3. To unmould the ice pops, dip the frozen moulds into warm water for a few seconds and release the pops while holding the sticks.

makes 8

fact

Watermelons are an excellent
source of vitamin C.

cals: 48   fat: 0.1g   sat fat: trace   fibre: 0.5g   carbs: 12.4g   sugar: 11.3g   salt: trace   protein: 0.4g

hidden animal products

Cutting out meat is obviously essential for a vegetarian diet, but so is being aware of what goes into ready-made foods and ingredients. Look closely at ingredients on ready-made products as they may contain hidden animal products. Did you know Parmesan cheese isn't vegetarian as it contains rennet?

Some common ingredients to watch out for are listed on the opposite page. Many of these have vegetarian alternatives that are widely available, such as vegetarian Parmesan-style cheese, so you can still easily whip up your favourite dish! For more detailed information about what is contained in ready-made products, reputable sites on the internet offer a wealth of easily-accessed information and advice.

watch out for...

Alcohol – can be made using animal products in the fining process. Look out for vegetarian versions.

Bottled sauces – check labels carefully as things like fish and anchovies are often included in bottled sauces. Worcestershire sauce, for example, contains anchovies but a vegetarian version is available.

Cheese – often made with animal rennet as a coagulator. Some cheese is naturally vegetarian but it is always best to check the packaging.

Desserts – check labels carefully as some shop-bought desserts may include gelatine, which comes from an animal source.

Jelly – most jelly is made with gelatine, although it is possible to buy vegetarian jelly crystals in different flavours.

Pastry – may contain animal suet or lard. Check ready-made pastry and also anything made with pastry like sweet or savoury pies, tarts and desserts.

Pesto – may be made with Parmesan cheese, which contains rennet. Look for vegetarian versions.

Sweets – often include gelatine, however there are a lot of vegetarian versions available that don't include gelatine, so look for these.

Soup – even if a soup sounds as if it might be vegetarian from the main ingredients, always check the label, as it may have been made with animal stock or fat.

chocolate fudge cake

prep: 35 mins, plus cooling and chilling
cook: 35-40 mins

175 g/6 oz unsalted butter, softened,
  plus extra for greasing
175 g/6 oz golden caster sugar
3 eggs, beaten
3 tbsp golden syrup
40 g/1½ oz ground almonds
175 g/6 oz self-raising flour
pinch of salt
40 g/1½ oz cocoa powder

icing
225 g/8 oz plain chocolate, broken
  into pieces
55 g/2 oz dark muscovado sugar
225 g/8 oz unsalted butter, diced
5 tbsp evaporated milk
½ tsp vanilla extract

1. Preheat the oven to 180°C/350°F/Gas
Mark 4. Grease and line two 20-cm/8-inch
sandwich tins.

2. To make the icing, place the ingredients in
a heavy-based saucepan. Heat gently, stirring
constantly, until melted. Pour into a bowl
and leave to cool. Cover and chill for 1 hour.

3. To make the cake, place the butter and
sugar in a bowl and beat together until light
and fluffy.

4. Gradually beat in the eggs. Stir in the
golden syrup and almonds.

5. Sift the flour, salt and cocoa powder into a
separate bowl, then fold into the cake mixture.
Add a little water, if necessary, to make a
dropping consistency.

6. Spoon the mixture into the prepared tins
and bake in the preheated oven for 30–35
minutes, or until springy to the touch and a
skewer inserted in the centre comes out clean.

7. Cool in the tins for 5 minutes, then turn out
onto a wire rack to cool completely.

8. When the cakes are cold, sandwich them
together with half the icing. Spread the
remaining icing over the top and sides of the
cake, swirling it to give a frosted appearance.

cals: 815   fat: 57.7g   sat fat: 33.7g   fibre: 5g   carbs: 69.5g   sugar: 45.3g   salt: 1.2g   protein: 9.8g

tumbling berries cake

prep: 45 mins, plus cooling and chilling
cook: 25-30 mins

350 g/12 oz butter, softened,
  plus extra for greasing
350 g/12 oz caster sugar
6 eggs, beaten
350 g/12 oz self-raising flour
1 tsp vanilla extract
2 tbsp milk

filling & decoration
525 g/1 lb 3 oz ready made
  buttercream icing
300 g/10½ oz mixed summer berries,
  such as raspberries, redcurrants,
  blueberries and small strawberries

1. Preheat the oven to 180°C/350°F/Gas
Mark 4. Grease 3 x 20-cm/8-inch round
sandwich tins and base-line with
baking paper.

2. To make the cake, place the butter and
sugar in a bowl and beat together until pale
and creamy. Gradually beat in the eggs,
adding a spoonful of the flour if the mixture
starts to curdle.

3. Sift in the flour and gently fold in with a
metal spoon. Fold in the vanilla extract and
milk.

4. Divide the mixture between the prepared
tins and gently level the surfaces. Bake in the
preheated oven for 25–30 minutes, or until
risen and just firm to the touch. Leave to cool
in the tins for 10 minutes, then turn out onto
a wire rack and leave to cool completely.

5. To fill and decorate the cake, cut out the
centre of one of the sponge cakes, using a
14-cm/5½-inch saucer as a guide, to make
a ring. Place one whole cake on a board and
spread some of the icing around the cake in a
3-cm/1¼-inch border. Place the cake with the
centre removed on top.

6. Fill the centre of the middle cake with two
thirds of the berries. Spread some more of
the icing around the rim of the middle cake.
Gently place the second whole cake on top.

7. Spread some of the remaining icing in a
thin layer around the sides of the cake. Chill
the cake in the refrigerator for 15 minutes.

8. Spread two thirds of the remaining frosting
around the sides of the cake, smoothing
it into vertical lines with the tip of a small
palette knife. Spread the remaining icing over
the top of the cake and decorate with the
remaining berries.

cals: 660   fat: 33.4g   sat fat: 19.5g   fibre: 1.6g   carbs: 83.4g   sugar: 61.5g   salt: 1.7g   protein: 7g

apple-sauce spiced cupcakes

prep: 40 mins, plus cooling
cook: 50 mins–1¼ hours

3 dessert apples

finely grated zest and juice of 1 unwaxed lemon

85 g/3 oz wholemeal plain flour

85 g/3 oz brown rice flour

2 tsp baking powder

½ tsp ground mixed spice, plus extra to decorate

115 g/4 oz unsalted butter, softened and diced

115 g/4 oz light muscovado sugar

2 eggs, beaten

225 ml/8 fl oz crème fraîche

1. To make the apple sauce, peel, core and roughly chop two of the apples, then put them in a saucepan. Add the lemon zest and half the juice, cover and cook over a medium-low heat for 5–10 minutes, or until soft. Mash until smooth, then leave to cool. Preheat the oven to 180°C/350°F/Gas Mark 4.

2. Put 12 paper cases or squares of baking paper in a 12-hole muffin tin. Put the wholemeal and rice flours, baking powder and mixed spice in a small bowl and mix well.

3. Cream the butter and sugar together in a large bowl. Beat in alternate spoonfuls of the eggs and the flour mixture until it is all used up, then stir in 150 g/5½ oz apple sauce (reserve any remaining for another time).

4. Spoon the mixture into the paper cases. Bake for 15–18 minutes, or until well risen and the tops spring back when pressed with a fingertip. Leave to cool for 5 minutes, then transfer to a wire rack.

5. Line a baking sheet with baking paper. Put the rest of the lemon juice in a medium bowl. Thinly slice the remaining apple, toss it in the lemon juice, then arrange it on the prepared baking sheet.

6. Reduce the oven temperature to 110°C/225°F/Gas Mark ¼ and cook the apple slices, turning once, for 30–45 minutes, or until just beginning to brown. Turn off the oven and leave the apples to cool inside it. Lift off the slices with a palette knife and cut them in half.

7. Top each cupcake with a spoonful of crème fraîche, sprinkle with mixed spice and put two apple slice halves on top.

top tip

These cakes make a healthy and tasty addition to the kids' school lunchboxes.

makes 12

cals: 247   fat: 15g   sat fat: 9.3g   fibre: 1.7g   carbs: 26.1g   sugar: 14.3g   salt: 0.3g   protein: 3.2g

popping candy cupcakes

prep: 30-35 mins, plus cooling
cook: 15-20 mins

115 g/4 oz self-raising flour
¼ tsp baking powder
115 g/4 oz butter, softened
115 g/4 oz caster sugar
2 large eggs, beaten
½ tsp vanilla extract
1 tbsp milk
pink food colouring paste or gel
40 g/1½ oz popping candy

to decorate
525 g/1 lb 3 oz ready made
    buttercream icing
pink shimmer sugar sprinkles

1. Preheat the oven to 180°C/350°F/
Gas Mark 4. Line a 12-hole muffin tin
with paper cases.

2. Sift together the flour and baking powder
into a large bowl. Add the butter, sugar,
eggs, vanilla extract and milk.

3. Beat with a hand-held electric mixer for
1–2 minutes until smooth and creamy. Beat
in enough food colouring to give the mixture
a mid-pink colour.

4. Divide the mixture evenly between the
paper cases. Bake in the preheated oven for
15–20 minutes, or until risen, golden and firm
to the touch. Transfer to a wire rack and leave
to cool.

5 Use a small serrated knife to cut a cone
shape out of the centre of each cupcake. Place
about 1 teaspoon of popping candy into each
hollow.

6. Slice off the tip of each cone shape, then
replace the cones on top of the popping candy
to cover completely.

7. To decorate, colour the buttercream pink
with the pink food-colouring paste. Spoon the
buttercream into a large piping bag fitted with
a large star nozzle.

8. Pipe swirls of frosting on top of each
cupcake and sprinkle with pink shimmer sugar
sprinkles.

cals: 357   fat: 15.6g   sat fat: 8.8g   fibre: 0.3g   carbs: 52.3g   sugar: 45g   salt: 0.7g   protein: 2.4g

wholegrain dark chocolate brownies

prep: 25 mins, plus cooling
cook: 30 mins

175 g/6 oz dates, stoned and chopped

125 ml/4 fl oz water

100 g/3½ oz plain chocolate with 70% cocoa, broken into pieces

70 g/2½ oz unsalted butter

55 g/2 oz light muscovado sugar

25 g/1 oz unsweetened cocoa powder

25 g/1 oz wholemeal plain flour

1 tsp baking powder

2 eggs, beaten

1. Preheat the oven to 180°C/350°F/Gas Mark 4. Line a 20-cm/8-inch shallow square non-stick cake tin with a large square of baking paper, snipping into the corners diagonally then pressing the paper into the tin so that both the base and sides are lined.

2. Put the dates and water in a saucepan. Bring the water to the boil, cover, turn the heat down to medium-low and simmer for 5 minutes, or until the dates have softened. Add the chocolate, butter and sugar and stir until melted. Take the pan off the heat.

3. Sift the cocoa into a bowl, then mix in the flour and baking powder. Add the eggs and the flour mixture to the saucepan and stir until smooth. Pour the mixture into the prepared tin and spread it into an even layer. Bake for 18–20 minutes, or until well risen and the centre is only just set.

4. Leave to cool in the tin for 15 minutes. Lift the cake out of the tin, cut it into 20 brownies and peel off the paper.

variation

Toast 55 g/2 oz unblanched hazelnuts in a dry pan, then roughly chop them and stir half into the brownie mixture then sprinkle the rest over the top just before baking.

cals: 106   fat: 5.7g   sat fat: 3.3g   fibre: 1.7g   carbs: 13.3g   sugar: 9.8g   salt: 0.1g   protein: 1.7g

sesame & cranberry squares

prep: 20–25 mins, plus cooling
cook: 20 mins

150 g/5½ oz rolled oats

55 g/2 oz sesame seeds

40 g/1½ oz soft light brown sugar

35 g/1¼ oz vegetarian mini
  marshmallows

70 g/2½ oz dried cranberries

8 tbsp clear honey

5 tbsp sunflower oil, plus extra
  for greasing

a few drops of vanilla extract

1. Preheat the oven to 160°C/325°F/Gas
Mark 3. Lightly grease a 28 x 18-cm/
11 x 7-inch baking tin and line the base
with baking paper.

2. Put the oats, sesame seeds, sugar,
marshmallows and cranberries into a mixing
bowl and stir. Make a well in the centre, add
the honey, oil and vanilla extract, then
stir again.

3. Press the mixture into the prepared tin
and level using a metal spoon. Bake in the
preheated oven for 20 minutes, or until golden
and bubbling.

4. Leave to cool in the tin for 10 minutes, then
cut into 20 squares. Leave to cool completely
before turning out of the tin.

top tip

These squares are best baked in advance.
They make a great teatime treat or
lunchbox filler.

makes 20

cals: 128 fat: 5.7g sat fat: 0.7g fibre: 1.3g carbs: 18.8g sugar: 12.3g salt: trace protein: 1.8g

chocolate chip & cinnamon cookies

prep: 25 mins, plus cooling
cook: 12-15 mins

225 g/8 oz unsalted butter, softened
140 g/5 oz caster sugar
1 egg yolk, lightly beaten
2 tsp orange extract
280 g/10 oz plain flour
pinch of salt
100 g/3½ oz plain chocolate chips

cinnamon coating
1½ tbsp caster sugar
1½ tbsp ground cinnamon

1. Preheat the oven to 190°C/375°F/Gas Mark 5. Line two baking sheets with baking paper.

2. Put the butter and sugar into a bowl and mix well with a wooden spoon, then beat in the egg yolk with the orange extract.

3. Sift the flour and salt into the mixture, add the chocolate chips and stir together until thoroughly combined.

4. To make the cinnamon coating, mix together the caster sugar and cinnamon in a shallow dish.

5. Scoop up tablespoons of the cookie dough and roll them into balls, then roll them in the cinnamon mixture to coat. Put them on the prepared baking sheets, spaced well apart.

6. Bake in the preheated oven for 12–15 minutes. Leave to cool on the baking sheets for a few minutes, then transfer to wire racks to cool completely.

top tip

Always cool cookies completely before storing in airtight containers, otherwise they are liable to stick together.

3

cals: 133   fat: 7.9g   sat fat: 4.8g   fibre: 0.8g   carbs: 14.4g   sugar: 6.2g   salt: 0.1g   protein: 1.4g

rainbow sprinkle sugar cookies

prep: 25 mins, plus chilling and cooling
cook: 10-12 mins

100 g/3½ oz unsalted butter, softened, plus extra for greasing

70 g/2½ oz caster sugar

100 g/3½ oz plain flour, plus extra for dusting

50 g/1¾ oz cornflour

1–2 tbsp milk

4 tbsp hundreds and thousands

top tip

Space cookies well apart on the baking sheet to allow room for them to spread during cooking, otherwise your cookies may merge together and you could end up with one large cookie.

1. Place the butter and sugar in a large bowl and beat together with an electric mixer until pale and creamy. Sift in the flour and cornflour and mix to form a crumbly dough. Gather together with your hands and knead lightly on a floured surface until smooth. Wrap in clingfilm and chill in the refrigerator for 30 minutes.

2. Preheat the oven to 180°C/350°F/Gas Mark 4. Grease two large baking sheets.

3. Unwrap the dough and roll out between two large sheets of baking paper to a thickness of 5 mm/¼ inch. Using a 6-cm/2½-inch fluted round cutter, stamp out 18 cookies, re-rolling the dough as necessary.

4. Transfer the cookies to the prepared baking sheets. Brush the tops lightly with the milk and sprinkle liberally with the hundreds and thousands, pressing them down gently with your fingertips.

5. Bake in the preheated oven for 10–12 minutes, or until pale golden. Leave to cool on the baking sheets for a few minutes, then transfer to wire racks to cool completely.

cals: 107   fat: 5.8g   sat fat: 3.6g   fibre: 0.2g   carbs: 13.3g   sugar: 5.7g   salt: trace   protein: 0.7g

raspberry & pink peppercorn macaroons

prep: 30-35 mins, plus standing and cooling
cook: 15 mins

175 g/6 oz icing sugar
125 g/4½ oz ground almonds
3 egg whites
70 g/2½ oz caster sugar
1–2 tsp natural pink food colouring
raspberry flavouring (optional)

filling
150 g/5½ oz butter, softened
70 g/2½ oz icing sugar
1–2 tbsp raspberry jam
1 tsp crushed pink peppercorns

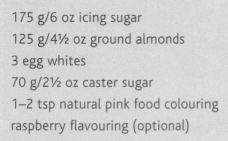

top tip

For piping perfect macaroons onto the baking sheet, make sure you have a large-capacity piping bag. A plastic or metal plain nozzle is also needed.

1. Preheat the oven to 140°C/275°F/Gas Mark 1. Line two baking sheets with baking paper.

2. Place the icing sugar and ground almonds in a blender or food processor and blend until very fine and evenly ground. Sift the mixture into a bowl.

3. Place the egg whites in a mixing bowl and whisk with an electric mixer until they hold soft peaks. Gradually add the sugar, 1 teaspoon at a time, until the mixture is smooth and glossy. Beat in the food colouring and raspberry flavouring, if using, until evenly distributed.

4. Fold the ground almond and sugar mixture into the egg whites, one third at a time, until the mixture is well combined. Spoon into a large piping bag fitted with a 1-cm/½-inch plain nozzle.

5. Pipe 40 small rounds, about 3 cm/1¼ inches in diameter, onto the prepared sheets. Tap the sheets on the work surface and leave to stand at room temperature for 15–20 minutes until a skin forms on the rounds. Bake the macaroons in the preheated oven for 15 minutes, then leave to cool on the sheets.

6. To make the filling, beat together the butter and icing sugar until smooth. Beat in the raspberry jam and the peppercorns. Pipe a little buttercream into the macaroons, sandwich together and serve immediately.

makes 20

cals: 157   fat: 9.4g   sat fat: 4.1g   fibre: 0.7g   carbs: 17.7g   sugar: 16.6g   salt: 0.1g   protein: 1.9g

index